LIKE A MAN

A Guide to Men's Emotional Well-being

Padraig O'Morain

VERITAS

First published 2007 by
Veritas Publications
7/8 Lower Abbey Street
Dublin 1, Ireland
Email publications@veritas.ie
Website www.veritas.ie

10 9 8 7 6 5 4 3 2 1

ISBN 978 1 84730 032 4

A catalogue record for this book is available from the British Library.

The examples in this book are composites drawn from many areas of life. They do not directly relate to stories of real persons. Moreover, they specifically exclude experiences described to the author by his counselling clients.

As with all self-help books, this book should not be used as a substitute for seeking appropriate legal or medical advice

Cover design by Paula Ryan
Printed in the Republic of Ireland by Betaprint, Dublin

Veritas books are printed on paper made from the wood pulp of managed forests. For every tree felled, at least one tree is planted, thereby renewing natural resources.

To my family
and to the memory of Tom Bennett

CONTENTS

HOW TO USE THIS BOOK

This book contains the fruit of many years of counselling men and of making my way – often uncertainly – through my own emotional and social world as a man.

I wish my readers well as they undertake the same journey and I hope this book will provide a sort of map to help them steer clear of avoidable pitfalls.

There are two ways to use a book like this. One is to read it from start to finish. The other is to dip into the chapters that particularly interest you. I have been both a straight-through man and a dipper, so I thoroughly approve of either choice!

Every chapter contains tips and these appear both in the body of the text and at the end of each chapter. They form a handy reference point and if you glance at them first, they will give you a taste of what each chapter contains.

The book ends with an appendix containing a glossary of key concepts to help you refresh your mind quickly on the main ideas presented here.

ANXIETY

Life's constant companion

1

In this chapter
- The unwelcome visitor
- Acknowledging feelings and getting things done
- The feel-good trap
- Two false friends
- The virtue of not knowing
- No, it's not awful
- It's okay to get it wrong
- The key technique: accepting anxiety
- Accept the catastrophe
- Paradoxical intention

The unwelcome visitor

George went to see a counsellor in the hope of getting rid of his anxiety about work, money and family issues. 'Why do you want to get rid of it?' asked the counsellor, who was a little unconventional. 'Anxiety is bad,' George replied, surprised, 'I shouldn't have it, I don't want it, it's ruining my life. I want rid of it.' 'I can't get rid of it,' the counsellor said. 'But isn't that what you're here for?' George asked angrily. 'Isn't that what people pay you for?' 'Actually, I can't get rid of my own anxiety,' the counsellor said, 'And I guarantee I can't get rid of yours.' At which point, George left without paying.

Anxiety is a more or less daily visitor to our lives. Sometimes it even climbs into bed with us, sits itself down at the table for dinner and trots along beside us when we go out to buy a newspaper. Who can blame us human beings for wanting to escape the nagging ache and the sharp pangs of anxiety?

Of course, we manage to forget our constant companion now and then: a good meal, an absorbing task, a funny movie or a conversation with an engaging person can make anxiety fade into the background. It does, however, come back. And because it comes back we need to know how to handle anxiety in our lives.

We avoid anxiety almost by default. According to Freud, the Buddha and many other thinkers, we tend to move towards pleasure and away from pain. There is nothing pleasurable about anxiety. However, the avoidance of anxiety almost always makes things worse.

How can it be that moving away from pain makes things worse than moving towards pain? The answer lies partly in the means we use to avoid pain and partly in the consequences of avoiding pain. Drink and drugs help to mask anxiety. So sometimes does frenetic, disorganised activity. So does putting things off that cause anxiety. So does avoiding people because of an anxiety about what will happen in the interaction.

As we know, the consequences of these activities can, in the case of drink and drugs, be devastating. Putting things off and engaging in disorganised, stressful activities is, let's face it, just as stressful as squaring up to the anxiety we are trying to avoid. Avoiding people because of anxiety over what might be said or done is frequently self-defeating and may well be unfair to them. Very often the thing that you fear the other person will be angry about, for example, is something that the other person is not even aware of.

Avoidance is particularly hurtful in cases of bereavement. It is by no means rare for a person who is bereaved to find that their acquaintances begin to avoid them. Indeed, it is possible to end up not only losing a partner in life but also the companionship of people in one's social circle. This is not due to callousness on the part of these people: it is due to avoidance. Neighbours and acquaintances, unsure of what to say, fearful of hurting the bereaved person, experience a little surge of anxiety whenever they see that person and avoid the encounter. It is not that they decide they will never have anything to do with this person again, but unfortunately there are cases in which that is the effect of their avoidance behaviour.

Avoidance can prevent us from doing what we need to do for our health and it can kill. This, I think, is a particularly male behaviour. The suspicion that there may be 'something wrong' seems to put us off going to the doctor. Pleas from relatives and friends to get the problem checked out are pushed to one side. Most men finally relent and take themselves off to the surgery, but for some it is too late and the consequences are fatal. Too many of us can recall good men who died because they avoided facing up to health problems.

On a less serious level, avoidance accumulates unnecessary tension in the one who is doing the avoiding. How often have you finally done a task you had avoided for months and found it was very easy to do? The psychic energy that went into avoiding the job was actually greater than the amount of energy needed to do it!

If you recognise yourself in this you are certainly not alone. As I wrote at the beginning, it is entirely understandable that we try to avoid anxiety. However, if we accept that the wholesale avoidance of anxiety is unhelpful at best and bad at worst then we need to learn how to manage it, how to listen to the messages it gives us and how to put our energy not into the anxiety but into the things that we need to do in our lives.

That is what the rest of this section of this book is about. The basic message is that we need to acknowledge our anxieties and to do the things that need doing in spite of them. Instead of hiding in a corner hoping anxiety will not find you, allow anxiety to accompany you if it must as you go about your day. In that way you will get more out of life and you will be of more use to those who are close to you.

TIP When faced with a situation that makes you anxious, ask yourself, 'Which will take up more energy in the long run: facing it or avoiding it again and again?'

Acknowledging feelings and getting things done

In the days leading up to the first presentation he ever gave, Derek was scared. In his imagination he could see his audience of senior managers sneering at him, perhaps even laughing out loud as he stumbled through his sentences. So Derek asked a colleague who had given many presentations to advise him on how to get his confidence up before the event. 'Stand up and start talking,' he advised. 'Sweat and stumble all you like. But start at the beginning and go on to the end. Then sit down.' 'How will that help me get my confidence up?' Derek asked. 'It won't,' he replied, 'but at least you'll get your presentation done.' So he did, and he was as bad as he feared he would be. But nobody laughed and the presentation was done.

Three steps
1. Acknowledge anxiety
2. Know what you need to do
3. Do it.

If anxiety is inevitable, then we must find a way to work with it. The three steps above suggest such a way. They are derived from an approach called Constructive Living, based on Morita Therapy, a Japanese psychology.[1] Morita's message is that we must acknowledge our feelings, including our feelings of anxiety. There is no need to run away from them or to pretend they are not there. However, while acknowledging our feelings – in this case anxiety – we must also know what it is that needs to be done in any situation. Then we must do it, even if our feelings are uncomfortable.

This is a simple philosophy but it can have a very beneficial effect on our lives. The key idea behind it is that we don't have to wait for our feelings to change in order to get things done. For instance, the alarm clock rings and I groan. I simply do not want to get out of bed and face this day or my 9 a.m. appointment with my boss. That's fine, the Morita philosophy would say, by all means feel that way. But get out of bed anyhow. Would you like to put that envelope containing your credit card bill through the shredder, unopened? No problem; perfectly understandable feeling. Hold on to the feeling but while you're holding onto it just open the envelope and see how much you owe.

Simple? Yes, but how many people have lost jobs because they would not get out of bed and face the day? And how many have lost homes, cars and other goods because they would not open the envelopes that brought the bills and reminders? Indeed, how many have never done things they wanted to do, have never gone to places they wanted to visit or have never asked for a date from someone they very much wanted to be with because they kept postponing it until the anxiety went away or until their confidence showed up – but the anxiety never went away and the confidence never showed up?

None of this means that you should treat your feelings with contempt. To do so would be to make a serious mistake. Your feelings may be giving you valuable information: that you need to prepare for the meeting with your boss or that you need to get your finances in order, for instance. However, feelings have a life of their own too. Anxiety can show up when there is no obvious or good reason for it. You can feel confident today and lack confidence tomorrow in quite similar circumstances. So while you enjoy your good feelings and learn from the bad ones, you need not allow them to dictate. Rather, allow them to accompany you as you go about doing what you need to do.

So,
- acknowledge anxiety
- know what you need to do
- do it

and as you get things done, good feelings are likely to follow in their train, as the next section explains.

> **TIP** When you feel anxious, just ask yourself 'What needs to be done next?' and start to do it while you are still anxious about it.

The feel-good trap

Steve doesn't go out. He'd like to and the girls at work have invited him out a few times but he's just not as good at conversation and at kidding and joking as the other guys and the whole idea of going out with the girls scares him. He tells himself that when he gets to feel good about it and about himself he'll go out with the girls, but not until then.

Roger would like to approach his boss about a promotion but he feels scared and anxious whenever the opportunity arises. It's important to feel confident when approaching the boss, he believes, so when he feels confident about it he'll do it, but not until then.

We always know how we feel so long as we are conscious and awake. Our feelings help us to navigate through our lives: we try to avoid what makes us feel bad and we seek out what makes us feel good. But our feelings can trap us too. They trap us when we insist that our feelings must be in harmony with what we are doing before we do it and while we are doing it.

Here is an example: suppose I want to go on a trip which involves making a journey by air. Now, I am one of those people whose feelings about flying will never actually be in harmony with flying. I fear that the plane will crash when it's taking off and I fear it will crash when it's landing. I'm not too crazy about the part in-between either. I have this feeling of fear despite the fact that I have flown many, many times. If I insist that my feelings be in harmony with flying before the flight and during the flight then I will never get off the ground. So I must accept my feelings of fear and get onto the plane. Otherwise I am never going to make that trip. In other words, if I demand that I feel good about the experience before it begins then I am never going to have the experience. *I need to be able to accept that the good feeling will come, not during the experience but after it is over.*

Think of a horse pulling a cart. We may imagine that the big, strong horse represents our feelings and that these feelings supply the energy that keeps the cart trundling along. The cart, perhaps, represents the doing of a task. So you put your horse in front of the cart, by feeling good about what you want to do, and off you go? Not so. Real life puts the cart before the horse: first you do the thing you need to do; then you get to feel good about it.

Have you ever gone through the anxiety of wanting to ask for a raise or a date or a refund? Remember how you only got to feel good about it after you asked? That's the cart-before-the-horse rule and it applies to almost all the important things we do in life. I really, really wish it were the other way around but it is not.

Another example: I have a negative feeling about making telephone calls. I don't know why and I'm not about to waste a lot of time and money finding out, but phone calls make me nervous. If I wait for my anxiety to be replaced by enthusiasm before I pick up the phone, then I will never make that or any other call. I need to accept my anxiety, pick up the phone and ring the number anyhow: put the cart (doing the task) before the horse (feeling good about it).

I have come across people whose entire lives are on hold because they insist on feeling good about a thing before they do it. Such people often cannot even get out of bed in the morning because, like most of us, they don't feel good about getting up when that alarm rings. Oh, they'll get up in the mornings when they feel good about it alright – trouble is, they're never going to get to feel good about it.

Life is full of tasks which you are never going to feel good about in advance. Much of the work of carers or of parents is like that. To go to another extreme, much of the work of actors in the theatre is like that: no matter how experienced they are, many suffer from stage fright before every single performance – but if they want the good feeling that comes with the applause they've got to walk onto that stage regardless.

Note that in all these examples I have said they accept their anxiety. If you are afraid to accept anxiety, you are in danger of spending your lifetime running away from it – into addiction or some other form of denial. What matters is to be able to have feelings such as fear or nervousness while you are doing whatever you have to do. You allow them to walk along beside you if they must. That way you don't deny the feelings but you get things done at the same time.

And if they follow the cart-before-the-horse principle, Steve might get a date and Roger might get that promotion.

> **TIP** Remind yourself that to get things done, you need to put the cart before the horse!

Two false friends

Michael's boss wants to see him on Monday morning. Michael's last project was two weeks late and Michael reckons his boss is going to reprimand him. He works on his defence all weekend. Michael is getting married in a few months and he really needs this contract to be renewed. He is unable to sleep on Sunday night and gets to work exhausted and anxious. But his boss has the flu and postpones the meeting until the following Monday. Michael goes through it all again and is a nervous wreck by the time he gets to sit down with his boss. His boss congratulates him on getting the project in with only a two-week delay and asks him to take on a bigger and more lucrative contract.

Can you read minds and tell fortunes? Do you, perhaps, possess a crystal ball? Whatever about the latter, mind-reading and fortune-telling are generally regarded as belonging in a carnival tent. Yet, we all engage in these activities in our daily lives and in doing so we often add unnecessarily to our anxiety levels.

Of course, a little mind-reading and fortune-telling is inevitable as we make our way through the day. When buying a birthday present for your girlfriend you will try to figure out what her reaction might be to various gifts. In other words, you will engage in a little mind-reading – though not always successfully!

If you look up at the sky before you go to work in the morning and decide to bring a raincoat you are probably doing a little bit of fortune-telling. And if you are a salesman then you try to 'read' other people's intentions and preferences, rather like trying to read their minds.

So there is nothing wrong with mind-reading and fortune-telling in their place. There is nothing wrong with them if you know that that is what you are doing and if you know the limitations of these particular activities. The limitation is that you cannot really know what is on another person's mind unless they tell you; that you cannot tell what the future holds until it happens. You can only ever imagine the future and you can only ever imagine what goes on in another person's mind – this is true even if you are a trained psychologist.

It is so easy to forget that mind-reading and fortune-telling have only a very limited use. Suppose you are writing a report for your boss and you expect she will not like it at all. That is fortune-telling. You won't know whether she likes it until you submit it and get a response. And if you submit the report and hear nothing for a few days it's all too easy to tell yourself that she is angry with your work. That is mind-reading. For all you know, she has been too busy to get back to you and she is satisfied with your work.

Of course, you may be right and perhaps your worst fears will come true. But how often has your mind-reading been wrong? Probably quite a lot, actually, if we could re-run a video of your life. Certainly in my case such a video would contain many embarrassing errors. Could you, like me, be like the philosopher Montaigne who said, 'My life has been ruined by a series of misfortunes, most of which never happened'?

Every time you react to what you think your girlfriend, your partner, your boss, your mother or the driver in front of you thinks, you are mind-reading. Every time you upset yourself on the basis of something that you believe is going to happen, you are fortune-telling. Just becoming aware of these tendencies, spotting them when they happen and then naming them to yourself as 'mind-reading' or 'fortune-telling' can reduce your anxiety levels.

You can also reduce your anxiety levels by becoming more comfortable with the concept of 'not knowing', as I explain in the next segment.

TIP Whenever you spot yourself mind-reading or fortune-telling just say quickly to yourself 'mind-reading' or 'fortune-telling' and break the spell of these impostors.

The virtue of not knowing

Mark made very good tables, chairs and presses but when a customer passed a comment about how very good flatpacks were these days, he got it into his head that people no longer liked the work he did. He brooded on this and became surly and resentful and lost business. Actually, the customer had been joking – Mark's work was highly regarded. Mark also became convinced that his wife and children thought less of him because of the decline in his business and he withdrew into himself for years. In fact his wife and children loved him very much and would have continued to do so even if he had lost the business completely. Mark's habit of assuming he knew what went on in people's minds had made his life miserable and brought pain to his family.

Information is power, they say, and as human beings we strive for information. The more we know, the greater our chances of survival. Countries at war rely on information almost as much as they do on guns. Bad information can render military hardware useless. The US/British invasion of Iraq was based on false information about weapons of mass destruction. The result was what is seen as a humiliating defeat for both countries though they possessed massive firepower.

There are also men who seek excessive amounts of information about their partner's activities – where she is going, what she is wearing, who she is seeing and so on. This is dealt with later in the book.

When we try to read people's minds, when we imagine that we know what they are thinking or when we imagine that we know what is going to happen, we are substituting fake information for the real thing. And fake information can be as devastating on a personal level as it is in military conflicts. When Anthony found a man's signet ring at the back of a wardrobe in his bedroom on returning from a trip, he assumed his wife had been having an affair. Ultimately his accusations and his anguish broke up his marriage. But Anthony's assumptions constituted fake information: the ring had been lost by the previous owner of the house and had lain there since before Anthony and his wife moved in.

The antidote to fake information is to get comfortable with the fact that there are things we do not know. Does it scare you to accept that you simply don't know what is going on in other people's minds or what is going to happen next? Well, the fact is that throughout your life you have never known what is going on in other people's minds – and they (thank heavens!) have never known what is going on in yours. So what is there to be scared about?

Similarly, throughout your life you have never really known what is going to happen even a minute from now. You may have made informed or educated guesses and you may have been right a lot of the time, but you have never actually known what is going to happen next because what is going to happen next belongs to the future and the future can only be imagined.

So you have lived all your life in a world in which you do not know what is in other people's minds and in which you do not know what is going to happen in the next five minutes. You are, actually, an expert in living in a 'don't know' world. What you need to be able to do now for the sake of your own peace of mind – or as much peace of mind as we can hope to attain in this world – is to accept that you do not actually know many of the things you have been telling yourself that you know.

You do not know that your customers are thinking rotten things about you any more than you know they are thinking wonderful things about you. And you do not know that your partner is going to leave you any more than you know they are going to stay.

Accept that you do not know; become used to the concept; become at ease with it instead of torturing yourself with fake information. And if you want to know what somebody is thinking perhaps you will then get around to doing the sensible thing, which is to ask them.

As for the future, it will reveal itself as it unfolds before you and will very likely be different to what you have imagined it to be. We can also help ourselves a great deal if we avoid indulging in what the psychologist Albert Ellis has called awfulising, as I explain next.

TIP When you find yourself speculating about people or the future, remind yourself that you actually don't know what they are thinking or what the future holds.

No, it's not awful

David was convinced he would become head of his department when his boss retired. He had worked towards this prize for many years. When a rival got the job instead, David told himself that this was awful, his colleagues told him it was awful and his partner told him on the phone that it was awful. In fact it was so awful that David got drunk and tried to drive home and hit another car. Luckily nobody was hurt but David lost his licence. Because he lost his licence he lost his job. Because he lost his job he became depressed. When you put it all together, it was awful. But just losing the promotion wasn't awful. It was painful and annoying and maybe unjust but it wasn't awful. And if David and his friends hadn't awfulised about it, he might be in a good job and in good health today.

Awfulising is what we do when we tell ourselves that it will be awful if such and such a thing happens or does not happen. It will be awful if I ask for a date and I am turned down. It will be awful if I ask for a raise and I do not get it. It will be awful if people are not impressed with me. And so on.

The problem with awfulising is that instead of getting on with our lives we are like rabbits caught in the headlights of a car, doing nothing useful and in danger of getting run over. Awfulising, as described by Albert Ellis (a founding father, along with Aaron Beck, of the cognitive behavioural therapy movement), is one of the prime means by which we make ourselves anxious and/or miserable.

You are on the way to work for a meeting with your boss at 9.30 a.m. The traffic is in gridlock. There is a very good chance that you will be five minutes late. It's awful, isn't it? That certainly is what you might be telling yourself as you picture your boss standing there with a face like thunder, telling himself how wrong he was to ever place you in a position of trust. But is it really awful? Before you start allowing your awfulising to send you to break speed limits and red lights and collect penalty points, perhaps you might allow yourself a more reasoned point of view. Your boss knows your record, knows about traffic and may very well be held up also. He will probably be satisfied with a quick apology and an explanation about traffic hold-ups. It isn't actually awful at all: it's just inconvenient. (I am assuming, of course, that you manage to get to most meetings with your boss on time!)

It is not awful that you have had a row with your partner. It is not awful that your teenager sulks and thinks you are stupid. It is not awful that the weather forecast is for rain when you wanted to go fishing. These things are inconvenient and annoying but they are not awful.

There are, of course, truly awful events in life, such as the death of a loved one, being seriously injured, your house burning down and so on. Unfortunately, there is a part of your brain and mine which makes no distinction between these life-changing events and the more trivial annoyances to which we are subjected every day. If you are held up because a car is sitting on a yellow box at a busy junction, this part of your brain would have you believe the delay is just as awful as your house burning down. But it isn't: it's a pain in the neck, it's annoying and it's inconvenient but it is not awful.

Of course, it is not just other people's actions that we wrongly classify as awful. We also have an irrational tendency to classify our own mistakes as awful, even when they don't really matter.

> **TIP** Next time you hear that voice in your mind telling you that this or that is awful, talk back and remind yourself that the thing you think is awful is almost certainly just inconvenient or embarrassing, no more.

It's okay to get it wrong!

A farmer who owned a donkey was going away for a week so instead of leaving one bale of hay in his shed for his donkey, he left two. This presented the donkey with a dilemma. Which should he eat first? Eating the biggest would give him a store of energy to take him through most of the week in case the farmer had not left enough, he reasoned (this was a donkey after all). Eating the smallest would still leave a good store of hay for him to eat later in the week and perhaps this was the wiser approach. But then, which was the biggest and which was the smallest? It was important not to get this wrong – his life might depend on it. He pondered and pondered, wondering which of the two almost identical bales he ought to eat first. When the farmer came home, he found his donkey dead from starvation and the two bales of hay untouched.

The fear of getting it wrong is one of the deepest that afflicts us. Human beings, after all, are problem-solving creatures. When you look around the world, though, you have to admit that we are not terribly good at solving problems. Indeed many of the problems that we struggle to solve were created by us in the first place.

The fear of getting it wrong applies not only on a global scale but also in our daily lives. Where this fear is irrational, it can add greatly to our anxiety. Which of these two almost identical jobs should you apply for and what if you pick the wrong one? What if you pick the 'wrong' holiday resort for your summer vacation? Should you offer customers a 6 per cent discount or a 7 per cent discount? What if you pick the wrong one?

The person who is haunted by the fear of getting it wrong can spend inordinate amounts of time making decisions and, once the decision is made, they may still go on fearing that they did the wrong thing. 'If I get something wrong, no matter how small, it will be terrible and I will be a bad person,' they seem to tell themselves.

Put that way, the irrationality of this fear is obvious. When you spot that fear at work in you, challenge it. Governments get things wrong and still get re-elected. Big business gets things wrong and continues to flourish. Your kids get things wrong and you still love them. So you need an antidote for this nonsensical fear.

First, you need to spot this fear when it arises. Then, remind yourself that nine times out of ten it does not really matter if you get it wrong. Usually, taking the wrong turn or buying the wrong jacket is far from important. People sometimes only realise this when confronted by a truly catastrophic event, such as a terminal illness, which puts things of this kind into perspective.

However, you do not have to get a terminal illness in order to put things into perspective. I would like to recommend to you two methods described by Susan Jeffers in her book *Feel the Fear and Do It Anyway* to combat the irrational fear of getting it wrong. The first is to think of results not as mistakes but as different outcomes. If you make a choice and it turns out differently to what you had planned, is that really a mistake or did your decision simply have an outcome other than the one you expected?

If you charge €600 for a piece of work and then discover that everybody else is charging €750, this does not necessarily make you a terrible person. For all you know, you may even gain a reputation as somebody who does not overdo it when it comes to pricing and you may get even more business as a result.

What really matters here, though, is to realise that you will inevitably make mistakes and that what really counts is to correct errors when you spot them. Taking this approach is the second method recommended by Jeffers. She uses the analogy of the autopilot on a plane. Planes tend to be flown by autopilot except when taking off and landing. As the plane flies along it will veer slightly off course many, many times but the autopilot continuously corrects the error. In other words, the plane gets to its destination by spotting and correcting errors. It does not give up and sulk when it discovers that it is flying in the wrong direction – it just makes the necessary correction.

This is the principle we can use to tackle our fear of making mistakes. The question then changes from, 'Will I make a mistake?' – you certainly will – to, 'Am I willing to correct my errors when I spot them?' So become sceptical about the fear of making mistakes. Notice how often others make mistakes and continue on their way regardless. Drop the myth that you can only be a worthwhile person if you do everything perfectly. Remind yourself of this: correcting your errors is far more important than avoiding them.

TIP When anxiety about making a mistake arises, ask yourself, 'How much does it matter if I get this wrong?' You'll be surprised at how often the answer is, 'Not a lot!'

The key technique: Accepting anxiety

George finally returned to the counsellor he had walked out on before. In the meantime he had tried all sorts of tricks to get rid of his anxiety and none of them had worked. 'You know, the Buddha sat under a tree all night trying to figure out the source of human suffering and how to avoid it,' the counsellor said. 'You want to know what he discovered?' George nodded eagerly, hoping that maybe now he would find out how to get rid of anxiety. 'His big discovery was that most of our suffering is caused by our attempts to avoid suffering,' the counsellor said and laughed. George walked out again.

No matter how many techniques we learn for dealing with anxiety, we will never get rid of it completely. That is why acceptance is hugely important in facing the anxiety-producing challenges and thoughts that life brings us.

Throughout the ages, thinkers in widely differing cultures have emphasised the role acceptance plays in living fully with anxiety. The Buddha believed that our attempts to escape the difficulties of life, which include anxiety, are the source of our troubles. In the twentieth century, Victor Frankl and Albert Ellis, two great thinkers in Western psychology, made acceptance part of the foundation of their approaches to anxiety.

What does acceptance mean? Acceptance means that I cease to fight with the reality of anxiety or with the fact that things are going to happen that I would prefer did not happen. Let us suppose that I am due to retire in a year's time. Suppose also that most of my social life has been built around work. My relationship with my partner is shaky. I have no idea what I am going to do following retirement. I believe my income will be inadequate. Under such circumstances, it would be difficult indeed not to experience anxiety. There is, so to speak, a certain level of anxiety that we could say 'belongs' to the situation I am facing. Working out the relationship with my partner, building a new social life, living more economically and finding new channels for my time and my energy: these are big challenges. How could I not feel a certain level of anxiety in facing them?

Acknowledging these facts as facts and getting on with doing whatever I can about them is acceptance. What is not acceptance is sitting there telling myself over and over again how awful it will be to be retired, how I will not have a penny to live on, how I cannot face living with the partner and so on. So non-acceptance, then, involves continually repeating to myself the 'awfulness' of my situation.

Similarly, if I begin to drink like a fish or to have an affair because while I am doing these things I can forget my anxiety for a little while, then I am also engaging in non-acceptance.

But what's wrong with non-acceptance? It so happens that non-acceptance is generally an ineffective approach to life. Let us suppose that things will work out just as badly as I fear when I retire. Even in that case, in what way was the brooding, the drinking and the affair of any help to me? The likelihood is that these behaviours (and brooding is a 'thinking behaviour') have done me more harm than good. Had I avoided these behaviours and instead accepted just the amount of anxiety that 'belonged' to what I was facing I might have saved myself much pain. Moreover, I might even have been able to figure out how to create a better life for myself when I retire.

To explain this better, let's borrow a concept from Buddhism and talk about primary and secondary suffering. Primary suffering is the amount of pain, anxiety etc. that 'belongs' to a situation. Secondary suffering is what we add on ourselves. Awfulising is an example of secondary suffering.

Let's say I am awaiting the results of a medical test. There is a certain level of anxiety that any reasonable person would have when awaiting such results. That's primary anxiety. The best I can do is to accept it and allow the anxiety to accompany me while I get on with doing whatever it is that I need to do. But suppose I sit there telling myself how awful it will be if the results of the test are unfavourable, how I might end up in hospital, perhaps needing long-term treatment – that's secondary anxiety. In other words it is extra anxiety, if you like, that I have added to the situation myself. I don't want to be glib about this – it can be very hard sometimes to avoid secondary anxiety. However, once I know about this concept I have a much better chance of limiting my anxiety to what is appropriate to the reality of a situation.

In effect, acceptance means being willing to live with the primary anxiety while avoiding doing the behaviours – obsessing, for instance – involved in secondary anxiety. Primary anxiety is not really under our control, but the secondary anxiety which we add on ourselves is.

How do we work with this knowledge? One answer is that we need to continually remind ourselves when anxiety strikes that we are willing to 'accept the catastrophe'. The next section describes what this means.

> **TIP** Acknowledge the anxiety that 'belongs' to certain situations, but tell yourself to stop when you spot yourself generating unjustified secondary anxiety.

Accept the catastrophe

I once knew a man who could not stand up straight because of a progressively disabling spinal condition. The condition also robbed him of much of his capacity to breathe independently. So he brought two cylinders of oxygen with him everywhere on a little trolley and breathed through tubes which went from the cylinders to his nose. He was probably the wittiest man I ever met. All conversations with him were punctuated by bursts of laughter. His disability was catastrophic – it killed him in the end – but he just accepted it and got on with things to an extent I have never seen in another human being.

In his work at the University of Massachusetts Medical Centre, Dr Jon Kabat-Zinn helps people suffering chronic pain or stress to accept what they need to accept while doing what they can do. What he teaches them to do is mindfulness meditation and yoga. His work has transformed the lives of many people, even though they still live with pain and stress. What these people have done is to give up their secondary suffering, as described earlier in this chapter.

One woman who underwent, in Dublin, a similar program to that used by Dr Kabat-Zinn, told me that the experience had given her back her life. She still had pain, and plenty of it at times, but the pain had become part of her life and not the whole of her life.

Kabat-Zinn has described his programme in some detail in a book called *Full Catastrophe Living*. The title is based on a line of dialogue in the novel *Zorba the Greek* in which Zorba asserts that he loves what he calls 'the full catastrophe' of life. He takes life as it is, the way it comes, with all its catastrophes and joys.

The Buddhist writer Pema Chödrön talks about the importance of accepting the mess that we are in. She does not mean that you should do nothing about the mess – just that there is no point in adding to your secondary suffering by denying to yourself that you are in a mess in the first place. By accepting the mess you can avoid the useless fighting involved in secondary suffering and get on with your life and perhaps even do something about those aspects of the mess that are in your control.

If we borrow something from Kabat-Zinn and something from Pema Chödrön we get the following:

> Accept the catastrophe. Accept that you do not know what the medical test will reveal; accept that you are scared of retirement; accept that you are ashamed of what you said in the latest row with your spouse. Perhaps there is something you can do about these things and perhaps there isn't. But accept the catastrophe and that act in itself will lower your stress levels and free up your energy for other things

Pema Chödrön also talks about a teacher of hers who, when asked how he dealt with his fears, said that he agreed with them. It is so simple and makes perfect sense and yet it is the sort of thing that one could go through life without ever thinking to do. Agree with your fears! Why not? Why fight your fears which are unlikely to go away just because you disagree with them?

So I agree that I fear the test result could be catastrophic. I agree that I fear I will not be able to get on with my partner when I retire. I agree that I fear I will get a heart attack before I'm sixty. I agree that I fear the company will close and relocate to a low-wage economy. My fears are my fears. Fighting them involves all sorts of secondary suffering – extra anxiety, anger and emotional pain. Agreeing with them sidesteps all of that extra suffering and again may well free up energy to do something about those things I can actually do something about.

Next let's take a look at a Western technique of acceptance and of agreeing with your fears, as developed by the Viennese psychotherapist Victor Frankl. It is called paradoxical intention.

> **TIP** Practice accepting your fears instead of fighting them. Then get on with your day.

Paradoxical intention

'I'm afraid I'm going to fail,' Mark told his father.
'Then get out there and fail,' his father said.

Victor Frankl, author of *Man's Search for Meaning*, developed the technique of paradoxical intention in Vienna in 1939. Following his release from the concentration camps in which he was imprisoned during World War II, he continued to use this technique successfully with a series of anxious and phobic patients.

Frankl's approach involves not only accepting your fears but exaggerating them quite deliberately. The approach is called paradoxical intention because it involves telling yourself that you intend to do something you really do not want to do at all.

For instance, we have all had the experience of waking up during the night, starting to worry about whether we will get back to sleep and then realising that the worry is keeping us awake. Frankl recommended that the way to get back to sleep is to decide to stay awake. How can this help us? He argued that it is the anxiety about staying awake that keeps us awake, and that deciding to stay awake removes the anxiety and allows us to go to sleep.

A paradox is a contradiction. In using this technique we contradict ourselves. How? By deciding to do the thing we fear doing – in the above example staying awake – and hoping it will have the opposite effect.

Frankl also recommended that we use humour in forming our contradictory intentions. He believed humour to be of enormous importance in dealing with psychological problems. For instance, a man who sweated excessively when he met people was instructed to tell himself, whenever he felt the anxiety about sweating coming on, that this time he would sweat at least ten litres of perspiration (clearly Viennese humour isn't exactly hilarious). The technique cured him of the problem which he had suffered from for four years.

Suppose you have a boss at work who is a very critical sort of person. You've probably noticed that if somebody is standing there waiting for you to make a mistake, you make a mistake. Using the paradoxical technique with humour would involve saying to yourself when the boss walks into the room: 'Boy, I'm really going to show him today: I'm going to make every mistake in the book – and more. I'm going to have him writhing in anger and frustration on the floor. In fact I'm going to make so many mistakes I'm going to make it into the Guinness Book of Records!' Do you see how this technique draws the anxiety and fear out of the situation by using exaggeration and humour?

You could use this technique with blushing ('This time I'm going to go as red as a beetroot – I'm going to light up the room!'); making telephone calls, which is one of my bugbears ('This time I'm going to say all the wrong things and really turn them off me') and with many other irritants and anxieties of everyday living.

It is, of course, important to remember that this is a mental exercise – you wouldn't actually set out to make every mistake you can think of in front of the boss and you wouldn't deliberately say all the wrong things on the telephone! Instead, you form the paradoxical intention to make light of your anxiety by *seeming* to welcome what you fear.

Frankly, it is impossible to explain in words why paradoxical intention works – but it does. Try it out on some small concerns and then on some bigger ones. See what happens.

TIP Practice paradoxical intention by picking some small inhibition and exaggerating it humorously.

THIS CHAPTER'S TIPS

1. When faced with a situation that makes you anxious, ask yourself, 'Which will take up more energy in the long run: facing it or avoiding it again and again?'
2. When you feel anxious, just ask yourself 'What needs to be done next?' and start to do it while you are still anxious about it.
3. Remind yourself that to get things done, you need to put the cart before the horse!
4. Whenever you spot yourself mind-reading or fortune-telling just say quickly to yourself 'mind-reading' or 'fortune-telling' and break the spell of these impostors.
5. When you find yourself speculating about people or the future, remind yourself that you actually don't know what they are thinking or what the future holds.
6. Next time you hear that voice in your mind telling you that this or that is awful, talk back and remind yourself that the thing you think is awful is almost certainly just inconvenient or embarrassing, no more.
7. When anxiety about making a mistake arises, ask yourself, 'How much does it matter if I get this wrong?' You'll be surprised at how often the answer is, 'Not a lot!'
8. Acknowledge the anxiety that 'belongs' to certain situations, but tell yourself to stop when you spot yourself generating unjustified secondary anxiety.
9. Practice accepting your fears instead of fighting them. Then get on with your day.
10. Practice paradoxical intention by picking some small inhibition and exaggerating it humorously.

Note

1. The Japanese psychiatrist, Dr Shomo Morita, developed Morita Therapy in the late nineteenth and early twentieth centuries. Morita Therapy was adapted for a Western audience by US psychologist David Reynolds as part of a Japanese-based therapeutic approach called Constructive Living.

PANIC ATTACKS

Reclaiming your life

2

In this chapter
- Panic attacks – not to be avoided!
- Mindfulness – staying with the experience
- Disputing
- Gradual exposure

Panic attacks – not to be avoided!
When Matthew was invited to attend his company's European conference in Paris, his colleagues congratulated him. The invitation meant that Matthew was in line for promotion. Matthew accepted their congratulations but inside he felt miserable.

Two years ago, Matthew had his first panic attack when he took a crowded train back to the city following a weekend in the country. Since then, panic attacks had hit him at conferences and in crowded pubs as well as on the train.

The panic attacks normally began with a surge of anxiety followed by a thumping heartbeat and shortness of breath. As these symptoms mounted during the attack, Matthew told himself he was going crazy, that he couldn't stand it, that he had to get away before anyone noticed what was happening to him.

Matthew had stopped taking breaks in the country, made excuses to get out of going to conferences and opted out of trips to the pub. The prospect of taking a plane to a conference which would involve entertainment and socialising was terrifying.

Matthew spoke to a senior colleague, Jim, whom he trusted, to say he believed he would have to forego the opportunity presented by the invitation to the Paris conference. He told him about the panic attacks. To his amazement, he discovered that Jim had also suffered from panic attacks in the past and still had them occasionally. However, Jim had learned to have a good career and social life in spite of them.

He took Jim's advice, booked his place at the conference and saw a counsellor to get help with his panic attacks. By the time the conference came around, he had resumed his previous activities. He knew there was a chance he would have a panic attack in Paris but he looked forward to the trip nevertheless.

Of all the unpleasant emotional experiences we undergo, the panic attack is, I suspect, among the most widespread. It is also among the most hidden. What is a panic attack? A panic attack happens when we misinterpret the normal symptoms of anxiety. Our anxiety levels rise and fall throughout the day for all sorts of reasons: a crowded street, being late for an appointment, shyness, even a passing memory of a difficult time. All these can produce surges of anxiety which pass away quickly and which are forgotten just as quickly.

Surges of anxiety produce various harmless though unpleasant symptoms. These can include:

- Thumping heart
- Racing pulse
- Sweating
- Shortness of breath
- Nausea
- Feeling faint
- A sense of dread
- Tightness in the chest.

We all experience these surges of anxiety from time to time, often for no reason we can pinpoint. Usually they come and go quickly without interfering with our lives. Sometimes, however, our brains misinterpret these symptoms as meaning something far worse is happening: perhaps that we are about to collapse, get sick or even die. It is this misinterpretation that throws us into a panic attack. What a panic attack does is take these symptoms and amplify them. That is what happened to Matthew when he had his first panic attack on the train.

A panic attack is the activation of your body's alarm system. It tells you that you are in danger and that you must escape immediately or fight for your life. In other words the panic attack represents the activation of the so-called 'fight or flight' response. This is a very good thing if you really are in danger. If you are on a stroll through the jungle and you encounter a hungry tiger who has you in his sights, you would be wise to escape up the nearest tree. And if your 'fight or flight' response had helped get you up that tree and to safety you would be pleased that you had such a useful alarm system.

The problem with a panic attack, though, is that it hits you when you are in no danger at all, frightens you and leaves you upset and bewildered. Why? Because you have, at some level of your mind, misinterpreted normal anxiety. You are going about your business, perhaps returning from a weekend break, as Matthew was, or having a chat with colleagues in the pub when your anxiety level surges. Your brain misinterprets what has happened as something far worse than it really is and triggers the 'flight or fight' response. Suddenly you are experiencing a panic attack.

What with the thumping heart, sweating and, above all, the sense of dread that accompanies it, a panic attack is, to say the least, an unpleasant experience! It is no wonder that people like Matthew avoid the situations in which they occur. The good news, though, is that the panic attack normally peaks and dies away within twenty minutes.

There are three really important points to keep in mind about panic attacks:

1. Having a panic attack does not mean you are going mad or that you have a psychiatric illness.

2. However unpleasant it may be, a panic attack will not physically harm you.
3. Other people are almost certainly completely unaware that you are having a panic attack, even if you are having it in front of them.

I wrote above that a panic attack will not harm you physically. However, the way in which you handle panic attacks can certainly affect your quality of life. This is most likely to happen if you avoid situations in which you fear you will have a panic attack. This can include:

- Avoiding the town centre or certain shops
- Avoiding certain modes of transport such as buses and trains
- Avoiding work or holidays which take you outside your home district
- Avoiding cinemas, theatres or the pub
- Even avoiding going outside your own front door.

What happens is that the person suffering panic attacks begins to avoid one or two situations in which panic attacks have occurred. An example would be doing your shopping locally instead of going into the city centre. Then you might have a panic attack in the cinema so you also begin to avoid going to the movies. Gradually the range of activities you allow yourself becomes narrower and narrower. Eventually perhaps you go from home to work and back; if you are asked to travel for your work or to go to a family event you suffer weeks of anxiety beforehand.

In this way the panic attacks or, rather, the fear of panic attacks, gradually tighten your circle of activities. In Matthew's case, as we saw, his avoidance of situations which might bring on a panic attack could have crippled his career and social life but for that conversation with his manager.

How can you reclaim your life from panic attacks? Fortunately, there are effective steps you can take but behind them all there is a key principle: *you must stop avoiding panic attacks and you must be willing to allow them to happen.* Remember, it is not panic attacks in themselves that restrict your activities; what is limiting you is the *avoidance* of panic attacks.

Let's return to that key principle for a moment, the principle that you must stop avoiding your panic attacks and you must be willing to allow them to happen. I want to outline three techniques you can use to help you manage your panic attacks so that they no longer rule your life. If you apply these techniques, you can expect your panic attacks to become far less frequent and perhaps die away altogether. When you have a panic attack it will be far less intense. Above all, panic attacks will no longer have the power to frighten you. Just like Matthew, you will be able to get on with your life even if you continue to have panic attacks from time to time. You will learn to allow normal human anxiety to rise and fall in the usual way as you go about your business.

These techniques are:

1. Mindfulness
2. Disputing
3. Gradual exposure.

I recommend that you use all three. Let's look at them in more detail now.

TIP Strange as it may seem, you can begin to tackle panic attacks by being willing to allow them to happen.

Mindfulness: Staying with the experience

'The first thing to do,' Jim told him, 'is to experience the panic attack fully.'
'But I already experience it fully – too fully!' Matthew protested.
'No,' said Jim, 'you run away from it. Instead of running away, I want you to stay and experience it.'
'But how?'
'Try mindfulness.'

Here is a common scenario: you are going about your business when you feel the familiar symptoms of a panic attack beginning to come on. Perhaps the you feel a spike of anxiety, your pulse speeds up or you become nauseous. The symptoms of a panic attack differ from one person to another. As soon as you notice the symptom you start up a series of thoughts about it. Here it comes again, you say. Everything I have tried has failed. What am I going to do if I faint or people notice I'm soaked in sweat or if I can't get off this bus?

As you continue to generate panicky thoughts you increase your own stress levels. Of course, you are already distressed by the oncoming panic attack; however, what is happening is that your thinking is adding a further level of distress to what is already there. You are giving yourself what we might call a 'thought attack' on top of your panic attack.

With your stress levels raised in this way, there is a good chance that the panic attack will be worse than it would otherwise be. At the very least your experience of the combined panic attack and thought attack will be worse than the experience of the panic attack alone would have been. This is a very natural and normal human reaction – but it can imprison you in your own home or severely limit your social and work opportunities. As we saw above, this is what happened to Matthew after he began to have panic attacks.

Now, let us see how mindfulness helps in this situation. Here is a brief outline of what it involves:

> When you are mindful you are aware of what is going on in reality in the present moment. So, you might be aware of traffic,

rain, another person's voice or your own breathing, for instance. A key aspect of mindfulness is that you don't get lost in a conversation in your mind. This is something we all do quite a lot and which, in many ways, prevents us from experiencing our own lives. Every time your mind wanders off into a mental conversation you just return to awareness of the present moment, without criticising yourself. That last point is important: while you are being mindful, you withhold your judgement as to whether this or that is good or bad. So instead of condemning the traffic or the rain or approving of the sunshine or the blue sky, you just notice them. (See below, at the end of this section, for a mindfulness exercise.)

What would happen if you applied mindfulness to a panic attack? First, you would notice the beginning of the panic attack, as before. But you would not engage with it. In other words, you would not go into a flurry of thoughts about it. Let me emphasise this: you would not get engaged in a distressing conversation with yourself about what is going on; you would not tell yourself how terrible it was or how frightened you were or anything of that sort. You would simply notice the sweating, the tightness in your body, the shortness of breath or whatever else the symptom might be. You would notice how the symptom changes over time, how it rises and falls in intensity, for instance. You would notice how it rises to a peak and then gradually drops away. You would also notice your breathing. As best you can, you would breathe calmly and steadily throughout the panic attack. You would avoid gulping down air because this could only worsen the symptoms. You would just notice your breathing and breathe as calmly as you could.

After a time, the panic attack will have peaked and died away. You will have stood your ground by avoiding the sort of panicky thinking that can make the whole experience worse than it needs to be. Remember, a key part of standing your ground is to maintain your awareness of what is going on and not to get into a scary conversation with yourself about it.

This is what Matthew learned to do. Whenever he felt that surge of anxiety, he breathed as calmly as he could and noticed the anxiety rising and falling. If the anxiety turned into a panic attack he simply noticed the panic attack rising and falling.

Mindfulness will not make panic attacks pleasant. You are never going to get to the point where you say, 'Yippee! I am having a panic attack, how wonderful!' However, if you lose the *fear* of panic attacks, and that is what this technique will help you do, then you can get your life back again.

It can also be helpful while a panic attack is happening to remain aware of what is going on externally. Be aware of sounds, sights, perhaps of the fact that you are walking, perhaps of what other people are saying to you. You can also be aware of your breathing. You will probably find that some kinds of awareness are more helpful and calming than others, so experiment.

A key point about mindfulness is this: practice it in your normal life and not just when you are having a panic attack. If you practice mindfulness, you will lower your general anxiety level and greatly reduce the chances of having a panic attack in the first place.

Mindfulness exercise
Here is an exercise you can use during the day to get yourself into mindfulness mode. It need only take a minute to do:

From time to time, notice your breathing.
Notice whether you are taking a long breath or a short breath.
Notice the little pause at the end of each breath.
Notice that the air is cooler entering your nostrils than leaving.
Notice your posture.
Notice the length of your spine.
Notice your feet against the floor or the ground.
Notice your clothes touching your body.
Notice the sounds around you and far away from you without getting involved with them.
Every time you drift into thinking, just return to noticing your body.

Mindfulness triggers

This involves using habitual behaviours to 'trigger' mindfulness. Choose one or two and then decide that when performing them you will maintain awareness of what you are doing, rather than daydreaming or getting caught up in fears or anxieties. Here are some examples:

- Using the telephone
- Going up or down stairs or steps
- Arranging your desk or other workspace
- Tidying
- Washing up
- Taking a shower.

TIP Use mindfulness to remove the fear of panic attacks even while they are happening.

Disputing

'Panic attacks really are terrible, though,' Matthew said.

'No, they're not,' Jim said.

'Well, they certainly feel terrible.'

'Actually,' said Jim, 'there are very few things in your life or mine that are terrible. But there are lots of things that are inconvenient and a damn nuisance and that's what panic attacks are.'

'You expect me to believe that?'

'No, but I expect you to tell yourself that.'

As mentioned above, what you say to yourself through the thoughts you think when you notice symptoms of anxiety can produce or worsen a panic attack. Certainly, before he had therapy Matthew's thoughts were serving to increase his anxiety and worsen his panic attacks.

Mindfulness helps to interrupt this process. However, in addition to maintaining mindfulness, you can help yourself by learning to think different thoughts. This is rather like having a conversation with yourself in which you say things that are helpful rather than things that make matters worse.

When you feel a panic attack coming on, you can remind yourself of three things:

1. that while a panic attack is unpleasant, it will do you no harm
2. that the panic attack will have come and gone within twenty minutes and perhaps even more quickly
3. that what you are having is a normal, temporary increase in anxiety which your brain has magnified into a panic attack.

So you could tell yourself something like:

> 'What is happening now is unpleasant and a nuisance but it cannot harm me and it will be over and done with in twenty minutes or less. It is just a normal rise in anxiety which my mind has magnified. I will breathe calmly and get on with my business.'

When you talk to yourself like this, you train your brain and your mind to look on panic attacks in a completely different way. Because panic attacks can be so upsetting, it may take a little time to get your brain trained in, so to speak. Use this method faithfully for a month and you will reap the benefits.

TIP Don't be at the mercy of whatever thoughts arise in your mind – choose to think differently when you begin to feel anxious.

Gradual exposure

On Jim's advice, Matthew started taking the train again. On the first morning he simply stood on the platform until the train pulled in and then returned to his car and drove to work, as Jim had instructed him. Even the arrival of the train had made his heart thump and had started him sweating. Next day, Matthew got on the train after the rush hour was over and got off at the next stop. There, his partner was waiting for him with the car. Gradually, he increased the number of stops he managed to travel to until – to his partner's relief! – he was able to travel all the way to work again on the train. He still felt a little panicky but he didn't mind – he felt he had regained a large measure of his former freedom.

Armed with the methods outlined so far, you are now ready to take back your life. Make a list in your mind or on paper of the places and situations you have been avoiding out of fear of having a panic attack. Consider how much each of these situations scares you and pick the one that is least scary. Now, deliberately go into that situation. When you notice your anxiety level rising, remind yourself that this is simply a normal increase in anxiety.

If the anxiety becomes a panic attack remain mindful, breathe calmly and think the thoughts outlined in the last section. Note the intensity of the panic attack on a scale of one to three on which one is mild, two is moderate and three is severe. Continue to go into this situation from time to time until the intensity of the panic attacks falls. Now pick the next item on your list. Again, this should be the least scary of the situations still on the list. Repeat what you did with the previous item.

Gradually you will regain your freedom to move around your world and to do the things that you need and want to do. For Matthew, the least scary situation was going into the pub, followed by taking the train. To prepare for taking the train, he began by taking a tram to work and learned to apply his mindfulness and disputing techniques in that situation before moving on to the longer journey.

As you move up that list, you may begin to tackle situations that you find very scary. In that case it can help to bring a friend with you the first couple of times you go into the situation. The friend could accompany you and perhaps later could simply be in the vicinity. For instance, if you are very scared about going into shopping centres, your friend could go into the shopping centre with you on the first day, on the second day he could wait inside the shopping centre for you and on the third day he could wait outside.

The principle is to reclaim your life by refusing to avoid having panic attacks. If you do this, your panic attacks will gradually ease. You will have them less often, they will be less intense and there is a good chance that they will die away.

TIP Regain your freedom by deliberately entering situations in which you feel panicky – start with the least scary situations and work your way up step by little step.

A note about relaxation

Relaxation counteracts anxiety. The more relaxed you are, the less likely you are to have panic attacks. However, we live in a rushed, crowded and anxious world. People find it difficult to make the time to relax and this may explain why panic attacks are so common. If I were to ask you to spend just twenty minutes a day doing relaxation exercises, there is a good chance you would find it difficult to put even that short period aside.

This is why mindfulness is so valuable. Mindfulness can be practised on the go, so to speak. Maintaining awareness of your breathing, of your surroundings, of your here-and-now reality reduces stress and increases calm. This in turn reduces anxiety and panic attacks.

THIS CHAPTER'S TIPS

1. Strange as it may seem, you can begin to tackle panic attacks by being willing to allow them to happen.
2. Use mindfulness to remove the fear of panic attacks even while they are happening.
3. Don't be at the mercy of whatever thoughts arise in your mind – choose to think differently when you begin to feel anxious.
4. Regain your freedom by deliberately entering situations in which you feel panicky – start with the least scary situations and work your way up step by little step.

BACKSEAT DRIVERS

The beliefs behind your feelings

3

In this chapter
- Sometimes it's all in the mind
- How we are influenced by hidden beliefs
- Uncovering hidden beliefs without therapy
- Albert's Top Thirteen
- Spot it when it happens

Sometimes it's all in the mind

When Martin got a big promotion in his company he felt an overwhelming sense of guilt. At first he believed the guilt was due to a conviction that he had conned his way into the new position. Everyone exaggerates their positive traits in job interviews and he, too, had gilded the lily. So strong did this feeling become that he was on the point of turning down the promotion – until his partner suggested he go to a counsellor for just one session. After all, she argued, the people who had interviewed Martin knew his qualities from experience and were well aware of what they would be getting when they promoted him.

In counselling, Martin uncovered his feeling of guilt about his father. His father had worked all his career in what he himself saw as a lowly position in a small company. Money had always been tight. By present-day standards, the economy had performed poorly throughout Martin's father's career, so changing jobs was not a realistic option.

Martin revered his father but was aware that he had worked for low pay for decades to support his family. What Martin now uncovered was his hidden, irrational guilt at doing better than his father. Martin's latest promotion made him higher paid and more powerful in business than even his father's boss had been.

Realising this, Martin was able to see that his hidden belief – that he should not do better than his father – was irrational. His father would have been delighted that his son, for whom he had made many sacrifices, had done so well. Understanding this, Martin was able to take his promotion and enjoy it.

Beliefs shape our experience of life. Most of us can accept that idea with little difficulty. We might shy away, though, from the assertion in one famous Buddhist text[1] that our minds actually create our lives. That seems like a step too far. My mind does not conjure up the car that goes out of control and smashes into me. Neither does my mind conjure up the board of directors that shuts down my place of work.

Still, the way I handle everything from everyday situations to life's challenges will owe much to my beliefs. We have all met the bitter man who sees life as a let-down. Ask him for the loan of a pencil sharpener and he will find a reason to say no, or he will give it with such ill grace that you wish you hadn't asked in the first place. Imagine what it's like for his kids or his wife! Then there's the man who sees life and people as basically good and who, because of that viewpoint, will go out of his way to help you. Clearly a more agreeable person to be around. Makes you wonder if that Buddhist assertion mightn't be right, doesn't it?

Whoever is right or wrong, perhaps we can agree that our beliefs have a massive influence on our experience of life. A belief may not make an opportunity come along but it may influence whether you see a possibility as an opportunity or a threat and whether you act on it.

TIP When you are puzzled by your reactions, look at the examples in this chapter and see if you can spot a hidden belief which might be causing them.

How we are influenced by hidden beliefs

Martin's belief that he should not outdo his father was just outside his awareness like a shadow behind a curtain. Yet it exerted a strong influence on his reactions until it was brought to light. But the moment it was pointed out, Martin had an 'Aha!' moment, as he recognised one of his oldest beliefs.

Let's make a distinction here between conscious beliefs and those which hover just outside our awareness. Could you write out a list of your most important beliefs right now if I asked you? Of course, but you would, naturally enough, be making out a list of those beliefs of which you are conscious.

No doubt, like most of us, you sometimes fail to live up to all these beliefs, so writing them down may bring you twinges of guilt. You might believe in the value of hard work but try to avoid it when the opportunity arises. Or you might believe in the value of moral courage but keep your mouth shut when a colleague is being bullied.

Needless to say, those beliefs that are just outside your awareness – like Martin's belief about not out-doing his father – will not be on your list. Yet these beliefs influence you too and if you breach them you will feel bad about it without knowing why. So if you want to make a change in how you experience your life, then a key step is to become aware of those hidden beliefs. Awareness of them will loosen their hold over you.

That may sound like a very tall order indeed and it would be if it wasn't for the work of the US psychotherapist Albert Ellis. Ellis has devoted much of his life to the study of how we are affected by hidden, unspoken beliefs. Later in this chapter I list the most common of these unspoken beliefs as outlined by Ellis. His work made him one of the fathers of what is known as cognitive behavioural therapy.[2]

Ellis insists that the way we react when something happens is influenced by hidden, irrational beliefs. Let's look at a simple example. Suppose I have a hidden, irrational belief that people ought to look up to me. Suppose also that I am in a job that requires me to serve other people. Perhaps I am a waiter or a doctor. Because of my hidden belief, I resent having to serve others whom I secretly, and all unknown to myself, regard as my inferiors. I am the rude waiter who slams the plates on the table; or I am the doctor who is abrupt with patients. Either way, people really, really don't want to have to deal with me. An encounter with me, whether in the dining room or the surgery, leaves them feeling upset. What they don't realise is that I may be quite unaware that I am doing this. All I may be aware of is a sense of irritation and resentment – but I may not know just how unpleasant I am or why.

But possibilities for change open up if I realise that running in the back of my mind is the belief that other people ought to look up to me. Once I see that, I can begin to understand how my belief shapes the way I relate to others. Now I can change my relationship with people. As a waiter I can be aware of my irrational resentment and serve the dishes with a smile. As a doctor I can spot the irrational impatience rising in me and speak to people as equals rather than inferiors.

> **TIP** When you want to change a behaviour, ask yourself, 'What belief would lead me to behave like this?'

Uncovering hidden beliefs without therapy

'I want to uncover my hidden beliefs,' George told the psychoanalyst, a man with a bald head and a white beard. 'How long will it take?'

'Hmmm, probably years,' said the psychoanalyst. 'After all, I expect you want to do a really, really good job of it?'

'Well, yes,' George said.

The psychoanalyst stroked his beard. 'Otherwise,' he said finally, 'you will be worthless.'

'You know, you're right,' George said, amazed. 'Hey, we're making good progress, you've found the first one already. Maybe it won't take years after all.'

'Oh yes it will,' said the psychoanalyst, grinning. 'There are hundreds more where that one came from.'

So how can I discover my hidden beliefs without spending years, and a fortune, in psychoanalysis? Luckily, Ellis has done the spadework for us. Through decades of research and work with clients, Ellis has brought to light our most common irrational beliefs. Hundreds of hidden, irrational beliefs are at work in the human mind. Ellis, you will be relieved to learn, has distilled them down to ten very common beliefs. And he has distilled these further to arrive at our three major, hidden, irrational beliefs. Here they are:

1. I must do well and get the approval of everybody who matters to me or I will be a worthless person
2. People must treat me kindly and fairly – otherwise they are bad
3. I must have an easy, enjoyable life or I cannot enjoy living at all.

First, does anything in the top three make sense to you? It seems to me that the first of those beliefs – I must do everything so well that other people will approve of me – is particularly common. All sorts of anxieties about performance, whether at work, in relationships or in bed, can be traced back to that belief. It explains why we sometimes fail to begin tasks – because we fear our performance will not measure up to our demands. It also explains why we sometimes fail to finish tasks. A task, once finished, can be judged and if we absolutely must have a favourable judgement, the prospect of finishing a task may be quite terrifying.

There is a key point here, though, and it applies to all of these beliefs: wanting to do well is okay; so is wanting other people's approval. *What is wrong is turning that desire into an absolute demand. And what is irrational is deciding that if I do not achieve my demand then I am worthless.*

So what can we do about this? Ellis, with vast clinical experience behind him, advises us to *turn each demand into a preference*. This immediately reduces our emotional investment in the irrational belief. So you might say:

> *'I would prefer to do well and to win people's approval but you can't please all the people all the time.'*

Now we need no longer be terrified by the possibility of failing to win approval – concerned perhaps, bitterly disappointed maybe, but not terrified.

How about the second major irrational belief – that other people must treat me well or else they are bad people? I suppose none of us wants to admit that this belief motivates us. But suppose another driver zips into 'your' parking space? Suppose a shop manager rudely refuses you a refund for a defective product? Suppose you bump into somebody on the street and he describes you as a 'stupid f****r'?

Now, each of these things is annoying in itself, to put it mildly. But don't we get annoyed over and above what is warranted by this type of behaviour? Don't we condemn our antagonists to all the torments of hell? And doesn't that, indeed, mean that in some irrational corner of our mind we believe other people must treat us well or else they are bad people?

Again what is wrong with the belief is that we treat it as a demand. Changing it to a preference changes everything:

> *'I would prefer if everyone treated me kindly and fairly but those who don't may be ignorant or upset rather than bad.'*

And what of the third belief? Do I really believe I cannot enjoy life unless I live under easy conditions? Perhaps fewer of us suffer from this delusion in its extreme form – but I bet you've met people who live by it. Some young men, at 30 years of age, still expect the mammy to put food on their table and a roof over their heads while they themselves lounge on the sofa and exercise the remote control. Others see red if the slightest inconvenience blights their day.

Actually, the desire for convenience rules us all. Marketeers cultivate that desire. The convenience store at the end of the road, instant loans, our willingness to buy ever-slicker gadgets only slightly better than those they replace – all speak to our longing for the convenient life.

So perhaps this belief drives us more than we like to think. But remember, the rational person *prefers* things to come easily. The irrational person – meaning you and I in our unreasoning state – *demands* that things come easily and condemns life or other people when the world throws up roadblocks.

So the rational version of this belief might be:

> *'I would love it if everything came easily to me but I accept that this will not usually be so.'*

We have just finished looking at the top three irrational beliefs which, according to Ellis, make our lives harder than they need to be – they weigh us down like sacks of stones.

TIP Whenever you find yourself insisting that things must be a certain way, take a step back and re-state your insistence as a preference. In this way you can begin to break the hold of irrational beliefs.

Albert's top thirteen

As I explained earlier, Ellis distilled his top three hidden, irrational beliefs from a list of ten – and he distilled those, in turn, from a list of hundreds of unhelpful beliefs that plague that rational creature known as man! Let's put the three beliefs listed in the previous section together with his list of ten. Here's the top thirteen – see if you recognise yourself in it:

1. I must do well and get the approval of everybody who matters to me or I will be a worthless person.
2. People must treat me kindly and fairly – otherwise they are bad.
3. I must have an easy, enjoyable life or I cannot enjoy living at all.
4. All the people who matter to me must love me and approve of me or it will be awful.
5. I must be a high achiever or I will be worthless.
6. Nobody should ever behave badly and if they do I should condemn them.
7. I mustn't be frustrated in getting what I want and if I am it will be terrible.
8. When things are tough and I am under pressure I must be miserable and there is nothing I can do about this.
9. When faced with the possibility of something frightening or dangerous happening to me I must obsess about it and make frantic efforts to avoid it.
10. I can avoid my responsibilities and dealing with life's difficulties and still be fulfilled.
11. My past is the most important part of my life and it will keep on dictating how I feel and what I do.
12. Everybody and everything should be better than they are and, if they're not, it's awful.
13. I can be as happy as is possible by doing as little as I can and by just enjoying myself.

Anybody to whom I have ever shown this list has read it with a shock of recognition. That 'Aha!' of recognition means these beliefs are close to the surface of our minds – close enough that we can scoop them out, like fish hovering just under the water, and take a look at them.

Now, imagine each fish has a hook in its mouth. The hook represents the part of the belief that's irrational. Pull out the hook and you get a rational fish! The way to manouevre the hook out of the fish's mouth is to restate the belief as a preference rather than a demand. Here's my shot at hook-removal:

1. I would prefer to do well and to win people's approval but you can't please all the people all the time.
2. I would prefer if everyone treated me kindly and fairly but those who don't may be ignorant or upset rather than bad.
3. I accept the enjoyment life brings me though I know it will not always be easy going.
4. It would be wonderful if everybody who matters to me loved me and approved of me all the time – but I'll settle for some of the people some of the time!
5. I would like to excel at everything I do but I remain a good person even when I am not Mr Perfect.
6. Sometimes people treat me badly for their own reasons but they are usually just imperfect human beings like myself who occasionally do the wrong thing.
7. I sometimes find it frustrating when I don't get what I want but I can handle it and I can get over it.
8. I can face life's difficulties and still feel good.
9. If a person or situation threatens me or frightens me, I will put my energies into doing what I need to do and asking for the help I need.
10. I can lead a fulfilling life if I face up to problems and take responsibility for myself.
11. The past shaped my life but today I can make new choices.
12. I accept that the world is the way it is and I get on with doing what I need to do.
13. My best chance of a good life will come from working for my own well-being and that of the people I love or care about.

Spot it when it happens
As Jack struggled with the evaluation report on the airbag testing project he headed up, he realised he would miss the deadline. Jack's mind immediately generated an image of his bosses in the head office complaining to each other about his failure to deliver the report on time. At once he started up a train of irrational thoughts: 'This is absolutely

catastrophic, they are going to be really, really angry with me. My reputation for top-class work will be destroyed. They will never trust me again. There is nothing I can do to fix this problem.'

When Jack realised what was going on, he replaced these irrational thoughts with something that made more sense: 'I really wish I could get this done on time but they know me well enough to know I'm a conscientious and effective worker. In any case, telling myself this is catastrophic is not going to get the evaluation done one minute quicker.'

Then he got in touch with head office, warned them the report would be a day late (the bosses had left town for a conference and would not even have seen the report had it arrived on time) and got on with the job.

When you take the hook of irrational beliefs out of the fish's mouth, as I wrote above, you get yourself a rational fish. Be assured, though, that the fish will reappear from time to time with the hook back in its mouth. When you are not looking, unhelpful thinking habits will re-assert themselves. When you spot them, remind yourself of the irrationality of the beliefs and replace them with more rational thoughts.

Awareness takes the sting out of irrational beliefs. There is no need to go around like the Spanish Inquisition exterminating every irrational belief you can unearth. Actually, the human mind resists that sort of thing quite well – after all, if you could change your beliefs at the drop of a hat, how would you know who you were from moment to moment? However, when you become aware of what is going on, by spotting the belief at work, you can gently put an alternative, more helpful thought into play. This process changes your behaviour and your experience.

Christopher held the irrational belief that anybody who did wrong should suffer harsh punishment. For many years, he did not know he held such a belief. But it troubled Christopher, a widower, that minor acts of wrongdoing on the part of his children made him so angry so quickly. He punished them harshly for offences that, in the larger scheme of things, simply did not matter.

On his daughter's sixth birthday, he sent her to her room for knocking her younger brother over as they both raced to the front door to get the cards the postman had delivered. She stayed in the room with neither cards, presents nor food until her aunt arrived to take the children on a birthday outing.

The birthday girl's red eyes told the children's aunt that Christopher had gone 'over the top' yet again. She stayed cheerful for the children's sake. She did not question Christopher about what had gone on. Perhaps she had unwittingly given Christopher the space to question himself – for as he watched the children, happy for the first time in many hours, walk out the door with their aunt, remorse flooded him.

To his dismay, he realised he had become a man whose love for his children was drowned in harshness. Fortunately, Christopher sought help and came to recognise the irrational belief that drove him and that he had inherited from a severe and joyless mother. This awareness enabled him to change the way he treated his children. Now, when his children 'make' him angry, he pauses and considers whether his degree of anger is justified and whether the punishment he has in mind is excessive.

He has learned to tolerate human frailty, in himself as well as in his children, and he is more at peace in his life.

We develop irrational beliefs as we grow up. We interpret our experiences and make up rules of living. Sometimes we have poor teachers. Sometimes we simply get things wrong. Trouble kicks in when we get so used to our irrational beliefs that we no longer realise we have them. Bringing our hidden beliefs into the light of awareness is one of the biggest favours we can do for ourselves and for the people we love.

TIP Be on the lookout for irrational beliefs, especially when you experience strong, unexplained emotions which don't fit the circumstances. Then challenge these beliefs.

THIS CHAPTER'S TIPS

1. When you are puzzled by your reactions, look at the examples in this chapter and see if you can spot a hidden belief which might be causing them.
2. When you want to change a behaviour, ask yourself, 'What belief would lead me to behave like this?'
3. Whenever you find yourself insisting that things must be a certain way, take a step back and re-state your insistence as a preference. In this way you can begin to break the hold of irrational beliefs.
4. Be on the lookout for irrational beliefs, especially when you experience strong, unexplained emotions which don't fit the circumstances. Then challenge these beliefs.

Notes

1. *The Dhammapada.*
2. The specific therapy developed by Ellis is called Rational Emotional Behaviour Therapy.

HAVE A GOOD DAY

Four crucial thinking behaviours

4

In this chapter
- Thinking is a behaviour
- Confusing intentional and unintentional annoying behaviour
- Insisting we are right at all times
- Using extreme language when we talk to ourselves
- Expecting ourselves to be above average at all times

Thinking is a behaviour

George is having a bad day – again. It all started when a car stalled on the yellow box on a busy junction when George was just ready to drive across. It was an old car and George was outraged at the idea that anybody would have the lack of consideration to, as he put it to himself, park an effing rust bucket in the middle of a busy junction. It was as if the driver was giving the two fingers to people like George who needed to be at work on time. Then when he got to work, his assistant pointed out a minor error in a report George had sent to colleagues for consideration at a meeting later that morning. Now George would have to tell the meeting that there was a mistake in the report. George blew up at the assistant for not spotting the mistake earlier. The assistant was too scared to point out that George had not actually shown him the report in draft form. This is terrible, George told himself as he made his way to the meeting. It is catastrophic to allow the people who will be at this meeting an opening to attack. I could be shot down in flames over this. At the meeting, at which his colleagues showed little interest in the 'catastrophic' mistake in George's report, a newcomer to the marketing department, fresh out of college, made a presentation which was applauded by all present, except George. Frankly, he regarded himself and what he had to say as being of considerable more importance than this new arrival with her fancy slide show.

Poor George is engaging in a whole series of thinking behaviours that, quite unnecessarily, make his day worse than it needs to be. Thinking behaviours often work at an operational level: they influence our state of mind and our actions but we may never have examined them deliberately and, indeed, they may have evolved so slowly or so long ago that we are unaware even of their existence. But when we become aware of them, we lessen their hold over us.

George engages in four common thinking behaviours which are, if you like, siblings of the hidden beliefs discussed in the previous chapter. First, he is reading all sorts of meanings into what was, after all, an accidental event: namely a car stalling on the yellow box at a busy junction. Second, he needs to be right, and to be seen to be right, about everything. This is an impossibility, of course, and as a thinking behaviour it magnifies ridiculously the effects of a minor mistake in a report. Third, he subjects himself to exaggerated forms of thinking that make matters worse than they need to be. He describes the minor annoyance of the error in the report as a catastrophe and thinks of himself as being shot down in flames. Fourth, he believes he ought to be above average in everything he does and therefore resents the newcomer to the meeting who steals his thunder.

I used the phrase 'thinking behaviours' above. It's very easy to forget that thinking is a behaviour as much as it is anything else. Sometimes we act as if we have no choice but to think the way we are thinking now. But if we look on thinking as a behaviour then we can hope to see it as something that we can change if it does not serve us well.

Let's look more closely at the benefits of changing your thinking behaviours. Suppose a colleague at work does you down. Suppose you confide in him that you are applying for a better position in the firm, an opening which most of the employees don't even know about. Now, suppose he sneaks in and gets the job ahead of you. You are going to be thinking some terrible things about this guy! Who could blame you? Even Mother Teresa would be thinking terrible things in these circumstances!

But suppose two or three years pass and you are still thinking bitter thoughts about him. It is a safe bet that by now this thinking has already damaged your well-being through keeping you in a constant state of anger. It may also have damaged your relationships. Perhaps people have grown tired of hearing you going on and on about what happened and have begun to look on you as a twisted, bitter man.

They may even tell you to 'get a life'. But in order to get a life you are going to have to use a new thinking behaviour. In this specific case, you will have to find a way to stop going over and over the wrong that was done to you. You are going to have to keep your thoughts on what is going on around you in the here and now. You are going to have to philosophise a little to yourself; tell yourself your life and your relationships are worth too much for you to go on with this kind of thinking, for example.

If you don't change your thinking you may destroy your life; if you change it, you may enhance your life. You need to be able to tell yourself that, in life, we meet some people who do us down and that sometimes all we can do is let it go and move forward. You may need to use mindfulness, as described in Chapter 2, to help you to interrupt the endless going over and over the injustice of what happened.

Two and a half millennia ago the Buddha pointed out that people who dwell on the injustices done to them cannot be happy. He recommended that we cease to dwell on old hurts. He did not suggest that the hurts didn't happen. Neither did he suggest that there is nothing we need to do to protect ourselves. But he suggested strongly that we avoid reliving past hurts if we want to lead fulfilling lives.

Let's take a more positive example. Have you ever met anyone whose thinking is such that they are less afraid of the world than their peers, that they see people in a more positive light and see themselves in a positive light too? Are their lives better than they would be if they thought in ways that were fearful and negative?

It seems to me that their lives are better even if their circumstances are the same as those of people who are negative and afraid. Their experience of life is better, even in difficult circumstances. There is a good chance that their feelings are also more positive more of the time. In fact, their lives just might be better than the lives of people who live in more favourable circumstances but who think in very negative ways.

So the way you think makes a crucial difference to your life and the good news for all of us, including George in the example above, is that you can change the way you think. And one way to change the way you think is to be aware of some common habits of thinking which can affect us and hold us back and which we may not even be aware of.

Let's take a look at some of those habits. These habits are the siblings, if you like, of the hidden beliefs described in the last chapter.

TIP Thinking is a behaviour – so if the way you are thinking hurts you, change it like any other behaviour.

Confusing intentional and unintentional annoying behaviour

George's rational brain knows that nobody deliberately stalls a car on a yellow box at a busy junction during the rush hour. However, the irrational part of George's brain immediately assumes that this is exactly what happened. George makes similar assumptions about the weather (yes, the rain waits for George to leave the house!), the government, strangers who get in his way, the photocopying machine that breaks down just when he needs a report copied – they're all deliberately frustrating him.

Every day people do things that annoy us: a delivery is late, the driver in front is moving too slowly, your wife slams the door, your daughter leaves her mobile switched off when you need to talk to her and so on. These things annoy some people for a few moments and then they let go of the irritation. Others, however, get very angry and stay angry for a long time. By and large, these are the people who assume that the behaviour that annoys them is being done for the purpose of annoying them: the drivers in front are laughing at them, the wife has slammed the door to upset them and their daughters leave their phones switched off to avoid talking to them, they imagine. In reality, however, very few of the things that annoy you are done with that purpose in mind. Usually, they just happen because people are forgetful or inefficient or are having fun when they should be working or whatever.

They're still annoying, though, and you may need to do something about them. You will find them a lot less annoying and you will deal with them more effectively if you realise that they are not being done *in order* to annoy you. It's the assumption of an intention to annoy that really makes people mad!

Take to heart – better still, learn by heart – an affirmation used by members of the self-help organisation Recovery Inc: *people do things that annoy me not to annoy me.* I recommend this slogan elsewhere in this book and it bears repetition. I have seen it transform people's relationship with the world in which they live. Try it and I think you will find it does the same for you.

> # TIP
> People do things *that* annoy me not *to* annoy me.

Insisting we are right at all times

George sees himself as living and working in an unforgiving world. In such a world, it doesn't pay to get things wrong. Therefore George believes he needs to be right about things all the time and that it is dangerous to be seen to be in the wrong. For this reason, people around George see him as arrogant. Inside his own heart, though, George isn't arrogant at all – he's just trying to survive in a demanding world.

Of course, I know that you, no more than George, are not the sort of tyrant who would insist on being right at all times! Actually this has nothing to do with being a tyrant. What it is really connected to is the fear of being wrong. In the chapter on conflict in relationships, I have outlined how this insistence can damage a marriage or other intimate partnership. Of course, the insistence on being right can be found outside the marital arena.

If a work colleague suggests a different way of doing things do you invest more energy than is necessary in defending your way? If your teenage son decides to get green highlights in his hair do you get into an overly heated argument with him over why this is such a bad idea? In an argument do you get angry if the other person fails to come round to your point of view? These are all examples of a sort of unthinking insistence that we are right and the other person is wrong. It's as if we are terrified to be seen to be in the wrong ourselves – though we may come across to other people as overbearing rather than terrified. By being aware of this almost automatic insistence on being right about everything we can improve relationships and our own emotional well-being.

TIP For a couple of days, try letting other people be right for a change and see what happens.

Using extreme language when we talk to ourselves

If the language George uses in his thinking could be recorded and played back, he would be shocked. Words like 'catastrophic', 'outrageous', 'shocking', 'fantastic', 'incredible', 'unbelievable' and 'fatal' litter his thinking. It's as if the verbal part of his brain hasn't moved beyond using a crayon to write words in big letters across the pages of his mind. His thinking is at the toddler level and this toddler has a small range of words – big ones for a toddler admittedly! – with which to express himself.

You reach for your car keys but they're gone from their hook inside the door. 'You are a complete, absolute and total idiot,' you growl to yourself as you march off to the kitchen to retrieve them from the table where you threw them last night. Your partner has a row with you and walks off in a huff. 'This is outrageous behaviour and nobody on the planet should have to put up with it,' you tell yourself. You've been feeling a little down since this morning: 'I'm depressed, this life is really a complete waste of time,' you tell yourself. And none of it is true. You're not a complete idiot for leaving your keys in the kitchen – you're just a normal, forgetful human being. It isn't outrageous of your partner to walk away – it's just inconsiderate. You're not depressed and your life isn't a waste of time – you're just having a few negative hours.

Why does this matter? It matters because exaggerated language like that in the example makes you feel worse. It threatens to throw you into a dark and angry mental world. It's only a choice of words, of course, yet it can change the whole tone of your feeling about your experience of life. So this really matters – and that's no exaggeration. The antidote to this kind of thinking is simply to give up using extreme exaggerated language in your head. When you spot it, stop it. This simple step can improve the quality of your experience enormously.

TIP Watch your language!

Expecting ourselves to be above average at all times

George seeks from the whole world the adulation he got from his doting parents as a baby. As a small toddler, George thought his performances – at drawing, singing, even waving his little arms about, for heaven's sake – were so excellent they brought out his parents' admiration. He didn't realise his parents were programmed to admire him no matter what he did! George has forgotten all this but he is still demanding of himself the above-average performance which he thought caused his parents to ooooh and aaaah over him all those years ago.

This behaviour is a twin of the approval-seeking mind-set described in the previous chapter. It can apply not only to seeking approval from others but to self-approval. Too often we expect ourselves to put in a superior performance when an average performance would be good enough. Now, it's great to put in a superior performance from time to time but the demand that you always put in an above-average performance carries a heavy price.

First, it can stop you from putting in any effort at all because you suspect your performance will fail to be superior. You are not prepared to settle for an average performance so you do nothing. It's like refusing to take part in a race because you're afraid you won't win it.

Second, it can make you disappointed even with a perfectly adequate performance. For instance, you're in a football match in which you put in an adequate, solid performance but you criticise yourself for not scoring three goals. This sort of thinking can take much of the joy out of life including joy that you have earned.

Third, it can stop you from doing your best. This seems contradictory, doesn't it? But if you're criticising and disappointing yourself because of your insistence on being above average you will find it very, very difficult indeed to do your best. Ironically, if you settle for an average performance as being good enough, you will put in an above-average performance from time to time. This is because you will be focusing on the task at hand and not on how you are falling short of perfection.

So when you spot yourself demanding a championship performance ask yourself whether it really matters on this occasion and if it does not, just remind yourself that on average, average is good enough.

TIP Quit working for applause – allow yourself the luxury of being average.

THIS CHAPTER'S TIPS

1. Thinking is a behaviour, so if the way you are thinking hurts you, change it like any other behaviour.
2. People do things *that* annoy me not *to* annoy me.
3. For a couple of days, try letting other people be right for a change and see what happens.
4. Watch your language!
5. Quit working for applause – allow yourself the luxury of being average.

NEEDS AND WANTS

Understanding motivation and change

5

In this chapter
- The needs that motivate us all
- All you want – your Quality World
- Focus on what is inside your control
- Total Behaviour – your point of impact
- How to cultivate optimism

The needs that motivate us all
John works as a salesman for Worldwide Widgets Inc. When he goes to work he likes to have a chat with the other salesmen and saleswomen about nothing in particular. Then he goes to his day's appointments.

He generally sees people in their offices because, if he can manage it, he likes to have lunch on his own – it is, he says, just one of his quirks. His wife rings him a couple of times a day, which irks him a little because she generally isn't ringing him about a problem – she just wants to talk. On Fridays he goes for a drink and a laugh with his colleagues. On Saturdays he plays a little golf.

At the end of every month he waits eagerly to see if he has managed to sell more widgets than his colleagues. He gets a big kick out of it whenever he's named top seller.

Also every month when his salary is paid into his bank account he and his wife work out their budget for the coming month. Just doing this exercise makes him feel anxious even though they have enough money to meet their needs.

Meanwhile he looks on in wonder as his sixteen-year-old daughter transforms herself into a Goth at the weekends and mopes around looking like the living dead with friends who look likewise.

We all need the same things but we don't all want the same things. As humans we share certain broad psychological needs but we each tend to have our own particular ways – our wants – of meeting these needs. In all, we have five needs which we try to meet even when we don't realise we are trying to meet them. One is survival and this is the one we share with all living creatures. The other four are psychological needs and we vary in the extent to which we share these with other creatures. They are: power, belonging, freedom and fun. If you are feeling frustrated, it is almost certainly because you are not meeting one or more of these needs. When you identify the human need you are missing out on, you can work to improve in that area.

Survival
This, of course, is the most basic need of all. John needs to go to work to get enough money to provide for his family. In other words he goes to work to meet his and his family's need to survive. Doing his accounts at the end of the month is related to meeting the survival need and his anxiety about this may be due to an ingrained anxiety that he and his family might be unable to survive. Doing accounts has this effect on people – except for accountants!

Belonging
The psychological need for belonging is so strong that most of us are constantly seeking connection with others. The family, the workplace, sporting events, membership of the union or a political party, chatting on the internet are all examples of ways in which we meet our need for belonging. John meets his psychological need for belonging when he chats with his colleagues at work and when he goes out with them at the end of the week. The most important area in which he meets his need for belonging, however, is in his family life.

Feeedom

John also needs freedom, autonomy, his own space and he gets this when he takes lunch alone. He also gets it if he goes for a walk on his own and he experiences a sense of freedom when he plays golf. My counselling experience would suggest to me that if you ever feel irritable or trapped the problem may very well be that your freedom need is not being met. This is especially so if you are very busy in your work or business life and also have many duties in your home life with no opportunity at all to unwind or to, as they say, 'be yourself'. If your freedom need is not being met you really do need to take steps to build some freedom experiences into your life, no matter how small they may be. I know people who go to work an hour early to get a little time to themselves or who spend time in their own room whenever they feel that need for 'space'. So you don't really have to sail single-handed around the world to meet your need for freedom!

Power

Power has a bad name, which is hardly surprising given some of the abuses of power that we see both on the world stage and on a personal level. But we all need power in the sense of personal power, a feeling of accomplishment, of being worthwhile. We all like the feeling of winning, either by ourselves or at one remove through, say, a football team we support. So, as Dr William Glasser, who, in his Choice Theory, created the classification of needs I am using here, defines it, the power need can be met in both good ways and bad. For instance, a sense of achievement can help to meet your need for power just as effectively as beating down the opposition. Meeting this need does not have to be about power over other people. Exercising power cooperatively along with others can also meet this fundamental need as can a sense of power within, which is often related to a feeling that one is doing things that are worthwhile.

John gets a sense of power whenever he wins an order from a potential customer. His big power kick comes when he's named top seller in the monthly competition. He also gets a sense of power if he scores a hole-in-one at golf. John would absolutely deny it, if you asked him, that he has a need for power. But like everyone else, he has; and like everyone else, he is attempting to meet that need in various ways all the time.

Fun

The need for fun and for play appears to be linked to learning. In other words fun, like the other needs mentioned here, is a genetic need. Babies and children learn and develop through play. Young animals play and in this way learn about hunting, chasing and other necessary interactions. And human beings play. We even tell jokes at funerals!

Going out for a laugh with his colleagues at the weekend is fun for John. So is playing golf and having a drink afterwards. His morning chats with colleagues are also opportunities for fun.

These, then, are our basic needs as human beings. Knowing about them, recognising that we all have them and acknowledging that we are all entitled to meet them in legitimate ways can change both how we feel about ourselves and how we feel about others. John's wife meets her belonging need by telephoning him even when there's nothing much to talk about. His daughter meets her freedom need by becoming a Goth and she meets her belonging need by hanging out with other Goths at the weekend. Note that John, his wife and their daughter all have different ways of meeting the same needs. They *want* different things although their *needs* are the same.

So we can summarise our needs like this:

- **Survival** includes food, clothing, shelter, money, reproduction and healthcare.
- **Belonging** includes loving other people, hanging out with a gang, following a football team, being a member of a nation, chatting to strangers on the internet.
- **Freedom** includes being able to make your own choices, realising 'I need space' and getting it, autonomy and independence.

- **Power** includes competing, achieving, doing what you believe to be worthwhile and leading.
- **Fun** includes playing, laughing, 'shooting the breeze', doing things badly (like playing terrible football) for the fun of it, playing games, watching TV and going to the movies.

> **TIP** Everybody you know has the same five needs – survival, belonging, freedom, power and fun – but each has their own way of meeting these needs.

All you want – your Quality World

Like any two human beings, Anthony and Mary agree on some things but not on others. That wouldn't matter if they weren't so aggressive about their differences. Anthony enjoys revisiting the parish he came from. Mary, whose family of origin don't bother to keep in touch with each other, regards Anthony's trips home as stupid and a waste of time. She makes it clear to him that this is what she thinks and they have had many rows over it. Mary works in a small accountancy practice, which she loves. She could do better financially elsewhere but she is too fond of where she is now to ever want to move. This really annoys Anthony who thinks it is absolutely stupid and wrong-headed to form such a strong attachment to a job when you could better yourself by leaving. This is also a source of quarrels between them.

As we grow up and move through life we develop thousands of preferences, likes and dislikes, ways of behaving and attitudes. We begin to do this as babies when we develop preferences for different foods, toys and faces (we prefer our mother's face, almost from birth) for instance. Some research suggests that babies begin to form their food preferences in the womb, from the food their mothers eat! As we grow up and go through life, we develop many preferences as a result of the millions of experiences we have.

These many preferences can be thought of as making up your Quality World, to use Dr Glassers' phrase. Your Quality World, then, is made up of everything that you want, everything that you are motivated to move towards. The preferences in your Quality World can range from the trivial – a Mars Bar – to the profound – world peace. Some preferences are helpful to us, such as sport or good conversation, whereas others are unhelpful, such as drugs or driving recklessly. We are always drawn towards our preferences, so a person who is 'into' sport is drawn towards playing or watching sports. Similarly, a person can be drawn towards drugs, and so has to make an effort to avoid them.

Because no two people have exactly the same experiences, no two people will end up with exactly the same set of preferences. Some of the preferences will, of course, be the same, but many of them will be different. This does not mean that they are bad or stupid; it means everyone has had different experiences to everyone else.

Partners' difficulties in tolerating differences between them lie behind much of the conflict in relationships. Conflict arises from the irritations and upset with which one person responds to the other person's preferences and behaviour. Sometimes that upset is justified. Sometimes, however, it just arises from each partner's failure to understand that the other person's preferences, i.e. the other person's Quality World, and behaviour will inevitably be different.

For relationships to flourish, each partner has to be able to accept that the other person has many preferences on which they both differ and that this is okay so long as they have enough preferences in common. Sometimes the other person's preferences make them impossible to live with (such as a preference for totally controlling people, promiscuity or other damaging behaviours). However, 99 per cent of the time, the other person's preferences are just different, not destructive.

What this means is that we need to stop trying to force our partners to become clones of ourselves, accept differences if we can and focus on what we have in common. You might think your partner's preferences are daft or annoying but unless you can get along with each other's differences you cannot get along at all.

Working through this issue of different preferences is a key stage in all long-term relationships. If successfully worked through it leads to a deeper, mutually tolerant relationship.

TIP Accept the inevitability that other people, including those closest to you, have different Quality Worlds with different preferences and try to tolerate these differences graciously.

Focus on what is inside your control

Jeremy grew up in a controlling household. His parents fought continuously over issues of control. His mother exercised control through a combination of bullying and blackmail. The blackmail consisted of taking to her bed for up to a week at a time if she did not get her way. His father drank in order to get a false sense of control, which he then took out on the children. Now Jeremy exercises excessive control in his own home. He tries to dictate what time his wife will arrive home from work and what friends she sees. He insists that their children follow rigid rules and gives no flexibility. Jeremy's wife has had enough of this. Shortly she will demand a separation. Jeremy's need to control has driven her away.

We try to control ourselves, people and situations to meet our needs or to get what we want. Often we are not aware that we are doing this. We may walk to the shop to buy something we want but be unaware of our surroundings as we walk down the street. Indeed, we may be 'a million miles away' in our minds, daydreaming about something, but still end up in the shop we wanted to go to: we were able to control our direction and our walking even though we were not aware of what we were doing!

Everybody needs a certain amount of control to meet their basic needs (survival, power, belonging, freedom and fun). To exercise control effectively we need to recognise what we can and cannot control. Then we need to put our energy into what we can control. We need to use control wisely and in ways which make our lives, and those of the people close to us, better rather than worse. Here are some approaches to getting healthy and effective control over your life:

Focus on what you can do and not on what you cannot do

You cannot make someone date you but you can ask them out; you cannot fix the lottery but you can buy a lottery ticket; you cannot make it stop raining but you can carry an umbrella. The ability to draw a line between what you can and cannot control is one of the most fundamental skills for living well in the social world in which we exist. It is by drawing that line that we are able to put our effort where it counts.

Surrender a little control when you can

Is your argument over which movie to go to really about the movies or is it a tussle for control between yourself and your partner? Are your rows with your teen over the state of her room really about the room or are they a reflection of your fear that you are losing control over her? In cases like these it can save needless upset – and can bring you closer to people – if you surrender a little control and go with the flow.

Never forget the power of asking

Sometimes all you control in a situation is the ability to ask. Asking is more powerful than you think and people seen as very successful often get that way because they have no inhibitions about asking for what they want. It's not in your control to make the boss give you a raise but it's in your control to ask. It isn't in your control to make a colleague redo a botched report but it is in your control to ask clearly for him to do it.

Respect other people's need for control

You need a certain amount of control but so does your partner; the boss needs a certain amount of control but so does the worker; the parent needs a certain amount of control but so does the child. If you fail to respect other people's need for control you may eventually lose them. You will also lose the cooperation that arises when people respect each other's need for control.

The way you handle control issues is of enormous importance in your life. Handle them badly and you can all too easily end up angry, alone or disappointed. Handle them well and you will have a good shot at living the kind of life you want.

TIP Focus on what is inside your control and not what is outside it; surrender a little control when you can; remember the power of asking; respect other people's need for a share of control.

Total Behaviour – your point of impact

Joe has two ambitions: he wants someone to share his life with and he wants a job that pays a decent salary so that he and his future partner will be able to afford their own home. Even in a healthy job market, however, he is not confident he can succeed in getting better-paid work. He has the qualifications but he doesn't have the confidence. He also lacks confidence about approaching women. When he goes to a nightclub, for instance, he cannot get up the confidence to ask a woman up to dance.

Joe experiences his lack of confidence as a feeling or emotion. He knows this lack of confidence is irrational. He knows that other people, who are no better than him, get better jobs and have girlfriends or wives. Joe believes these other men have what he wants because they are confident. From this he draws the conclusion that if he becomes confident, he can have these things too.

The good news for Joe is that he doesn't have to wait for his confidence to arrive before he sets about getting what he wants. While some of the men he envies are confident people, others are not. But even those who are not confident went ahead and applied for better jobs and asked people out on dates. They felt really uncertain when they did it and some of them went through agonies of embarrassment. But they did it anyway and that's what got them what they wanted.

Like Joe, many people make the mistake of postponing action until after they become confident about the thing they want to do. The fact is, it is almost impossible to become confident until after you have done it! To get a job it is more important to apply for it than it is to be confident about your prospects; to get a date it is more important to ask for it than it is to be confident about your chances.

To understand this more clearly, let's look at the concept of Total Behaviour as defined by Dr Glasser in his books on *Reality Therapy and Choice Theory*. The concept of Total Behaviour is based on the fact that at any one time, even if all you are doing is sitting reading this book, four things are going on for you.

First, you are doing something: namely reading this book. Second, you are thinking: perhaps about what you are reading or perhaps about something completely different. Third, you are experiencing feelings: calm, anxiety, interest, boredom, whatever. Fourth, you are having a physiological experience: your heart is beating at a certain rate; you are alert or sluggish and so on.

All your behaviour, at any time, is made up of these four components: doing, thinking, feeling and physiological events. Some of these components of your Total Behaviour are very much under your control; others are not. In particular, it is important to understand that you cannot directly control your feelings.

If you could directly control your feelings you would never have a bad day again, would you? You could lose your job and your home could burn down and your car could get clamped all on the same day and you'd feel fantastic because you could simply choose to feel that way! That, as we all know to our cost, is not how it works.

So you cannot control your feelings. And if you cannot control your feelings, then waiting for them to change before you take action is a poor strategy, as Joe is in danger of finding out. Your feelings will change alright but not at a time of your choosing. They're like the Irish weather: you can't rely on them and you can't forecast them with accuracy.

The other thing you cannot change directly is your physiology. If you're sitting there like a stranded whale on the sofa feeling really, really tired you can't command yourself to feel light and alert and achieve it, just like that. I know – I've tried!

What can you control? You can control your thinking, to a certain extent. You can decide to think about something cheerful or something sad, you can tell yourself stories about how wonderful or awful people are and you can philosophise to yourself about life and its problems. You can give out to yourself, analyse situations and indulge in fantasy. You can also use the many helpful approaches to thinking which you will find in the remainder of this chapter and this book.

When I was growing up, my father sometimes had to move sheep from one field to another by walking them along the road. Now, sheep will go where you want them to go – until they get caught up in the idea of going somewhere else. A gateway, a gap in the hedge, a ditch are all likely to capture their attention. So suddenly, instead of moving them along the road, you're trying to get them out of someone else's field or garden.

Our thoughts are like that – they have a habit of drifting off and of winding up where they are not supposed to be. So your control of your thinking is never complete. Nevertheless, the fact remains that your thinking is controllable to an extent that is never true of your feelings or your physiology. What you can control most of all, though, is what you *do*. You can *make* a telephone call, *get out* of bed in the morning, *work*, *exercise* and *do* a million other things *regardless of how you feel.*

Joe believes that as soon as his feelings change, he will be ready to look for a better job or ask a woman out on a date. However, as I pointed out earlier, Joe doesn't need to change his feelings: he needs to change what he does. In other words, he needs to ask for that job or that date even while he is still feeling scared about it.

Making that change in what he does will require a change in how he thinks. Joe needs to persuade himself that he should take action instead of becoming a prisoner of his feelings and it is through his thinking that he is likely to persuade himself. If Joe makes that change, there is a good chance that he will feel better. There is even a good chance that his confidence will grow!

Does this mean I am saying that, in some way, feelings are bad? No, I most certainly am not. Your feelings tell you that you are happy or unhappy with a situation. Allowing yourself to be fully aware of your feelings is one of the greatest gifts you can give yourself. However, it is action that brings about change: forgiving a child though you feel angry; climbing out of bed though you feel tired; asking for a pay-rise though you feel scared; walking yourself into the doctor's surgery though you feel embarrassed. And notice what happens: there is a good chance you will feel glad you forgave the child; energised after you get up; happy with yourself that you asked for that pay-rise; relieved when you leave the doctor's surgery.

There is a key principle in here: generally speaking you get to feel good about doing something after you do it, not before.

> **TIP** Change what you do or what you think without waiting for your feelings to change.

How to cultivate optimism

John and Martin would like to win the lottery. John is an optimist and Martin is a pessimist. John wins the lottery. Martin does not. John does not win the lottery because he is an optimist – he wins it because he bought a ticket and the numbers came up. But he bought the ticket because he is an optimist. Martin did not fail to win the lottery because he is a pessimist; however, because he is a pessimist he never bothered to buy a ticket, and because he never bothered to buy a ticket he never had a chance of winning.

The pioneering work on optimism has been done by Dr Martin Seligman in the United States. Seligman's interest is in studying the positive aspects of human psychology. What makes us happy, successful, resilient? he asks.

Seligman has conducted extensive research in his bid to answer this question. As part of this research, he has tested the optimism levels of workers employed to sell insurance over the phone – a very tough job indeed. He found that, over time, even when you allow for all other factors, those who are optimistic at the start are more likely to last in the job than those who are pessimistic. He also found that the optimists sell more insurance than the pessimists.

Seligman also found that people who are optimistic are seen as more attractive than others. Unfair? Sure, but don't go getting all pessimistic about it! Instead, take a look at Seligman's advice on how to cultivate optimism.

The three most important things to do, Seligman found, are these: replace negative global judgements with specific judgements (I'll explain this mouthful below), give yourself fixable reasons for what goes wrong and give yourself the credit for what goes right. Let's look more closely at these three pieces of advice and what they mean.

Replace negative global judgements with specific judgements

A global judgement is an overall judgement about yourself. 'Women don't like me', 'I'm just no good at maths', 'I'm a born failure' – these are all examples of global judgements.

If you're making negative global judgements about yourself it's very, very difficult to move forward. If you believe 'Women don't like me' it's awfully hard to ask for a date. If you believe 'I'm no good at maths' you will find it difficult to prepare for an exam or even to take up the subject. If you believe 'I'm a born failure' you will be terrified to take up a challenge. What you need to do is to spot these negative global judgements and change them to specific judgements. A specific judgement would be 'Some women like me and some women don't'. The global judgement left no way out: women don't like me and that's that. The specific judgement offers a way forward: find the women who like you.

Using this approach, 'I'm no good at maths' becomes 'Sometimes I'm good at maths and sometimes not' or 'I haven't yet found the way to do maths that suits me'; 'I'm a born failure' becomes 'Sometimes I succeed and sometimes I fail' or 'So far I've had more failure than success in my life'. That last thought may not be a very comforting one but it's a lot better than telling yourself that you're a born failure.

You could call this the *Sometimes this, sometimes that* attitude: sometimes I'm good, sometimes I'm bad; sometimes I'm clever, sometimes I'm a fool; sometimes I'm happy, sometimes I'm sad; sometimes I'm calm, sometimes I'm mad!

Give yourself fixable reasons for what goes wrong
'I didn't pass because I'm stupid' is an unfixable reason for your failure in an exam. 'I failed the exam because I didn't revise enough' is fixable: next time, revise more.

'Nobody wants to buy what I'm selling' is unfixable unless you change the product. 'The last three people I rang didn't buy my product, so I'm three people closer to the one who will' is a fixable reason. This is the sort of reasoning Seligman found in successful insurance salespersons whose job was to telephone households out of the blue to try to sell policies.

'I have a depressive personality so I'm never going to feel better' is another unfixable reason, in this case for feeling down. 'My present way of thinking makes it easier for me to become depressed' is fixable: change your way of thinking.

Give yourself credit for what goes right

Many of us find ways to discount our achievements when things go right. 'I only got the job because they couldn't find who they wanted at the time' is one example; 'Sure, the kids like to see me – they like the money they get from me' is another. We find ways to turn away compliments from others. Complimented on doing a great selling job we will say, 'Ah, they were ready to buy'.

To generate optimism we need to be kinder to ourselves in these situations. 'I got the job because of my experience and because I did a good interview' is a thought which acknowledges your own good qualities. 'The kids love to see me because I'm their Dad' will do far more for your optimism and general mental health than the toxic notion that they are only interested in your money. And a simple 'Thank you' is a healthy response to a compliment, and a response, moreover, which suggests you deserve the compliment.

Optimism is good for you – if you are not naturally optimistic you may have to work at these ways of generating optimism but it's work that will give you a return that's well worth the effort.

TIP Begin to generate optimism by avoiding sweeping negative statements about yourself and by giving yourself the credit when things go right.

THIS CHAPTER'S TIPS

1. Everybody you know has the same five needs – survival, belonging, freedom, power and fun – but each has their own way of meeting these needs.
2. Accept the inevitability that other people, including those closest to you, have different Quality Worlds with different preferences and try to tolerate these differences graciously.
3. Focus on what is inside your control and not what is outside it; surrender a little control when you can; remember the power of asking; respect other people's need for a share of control.
4. Change what you do or what you think without waiting for your feelings to change.
5. Begin to generate optimism by avoiding sweeping negative statements about yourself and by giving yourself the credit when things go right.

THE BLUES

Confronting depression and weakening its hold

6

In this chapter
- Depression's three allies
- Brooding is bad for you!
- Maintain energy to improve your mood
- Become aware of how depression 'hooks' you
- What good is talk?
- Creating a better morning routine
- Advice from Japan
- Working with your Total Behaviour
- Cultivate gratitude to fight the blues

Depression's three allies

Gerald is an intelligent, likeable young man who had everything to look forward to when he had his first serious bout of depression at nineteen. The depression floored him. He lost his energy, his feelings were extraordinarily bleak and even thinking was an effort. He gave up college and took to his bed. His worried parents looked after him. They called in the family GP who prescribed an anti-depressant.

Gerald's depression lifted after a few weeks and he got a part-time job. He intended to go back to college at the start of the next academic year. His great fear was that the depression would return. It came back one morning, a couple of months later. His energy level fell and he took to staying in bed all day. He never returned to his part-time job.

This became Gerald's pattern: depression, recovery, fear, depression. The pattern disrupted his attempts to get on with his life time and again. The intervals shortened between bouts of depression. He came to see himself as suffering from an incurable 'clinical depression'. Life looked bleak.

Everybody who is normal has experienced depression. If we are lucky, our depression lifts after a few hours or a few days; we remember it as 'a touch of the blues' and we get on with our lives. If we are unlucky, the depression 'sticks' and can last for a long time. When that happens we may be helped by going to a counsellor or we may find that the depression eventually lifts of its own accord or when our circumstances change. What none of us wants, though, is for the depression to return. Of course, we know that we will still get the occasional bout of the blues but we really do not want ever again to experience that knock-out depression that takes the joy out of life for an unpredictable period of time.

This chapter aims to help you reduce the chances that a serious depression will re-occur. If you have not experienced a serious depression it will help you to deal with the blues more effectively than before and will reduce both the frequency and the length of time you suffer from them.

Let's begin by looking at a triad of symptoms usually involved in depression. These are low mood, negative thoughts and low energy. We could call these depression's three allies because if we misinterpret these symptoms when they come along, we can actually make ourselves depressed. Misinterpreting these symptoms means assuming that if any one of them arises then we are in for a bout of deep depression. Such a misinterpretation can, in itself, bring on a depression.

A deep depression, as I mentioned above, generally involves a combination of all three symptoms. But you can also have one or more of these symptoms without being depressed. For instance, anybody can feel fed up, 'down' and 'low' for a few hours or even a couple of days. A dark, rainy, cold day will do that for most of us. Equally, we all go through periods when we feel fatigued. After a little while, the dark mood and thoughts or the fatigue pass.

However, a person who has suffered some bouts of deep depression can link all these symptoms in his mind. Then, when he experiences one of the symptoms in the future, he may well assume that the full depression is back. The way he reacts to this assumption may actually create the depression.

Look at Gerald's story again:

Gerald's depression-free bouts usually end when he wakes up in the morning in an unexpectedly low mood. Gerald's heart sinks when he notices the arrival of the low mood. He immediately subjects himself to what writer Richard Carlson has called a 'thought attack'. The depression is back, he tells himself. All his attempts to avoid it have failed. Nothing works. His efforts are useless. He is in a tunnel from which there is no escape.

He decides he cannot face work and stays in bed. When he eventually gets up, he feels fatigued, as you do when you stay in bed too long. He now has all the components of depression in place: low mood, negative thoughts and low energy.

Gerald woke up in a low mood because during the night he had a depressing dream. Perhaps you have experienced this yourself: a bleak and depressing dream or nightmare which drags you down for the day. But we forget most of our dreams, so let's assume Gerald doesn't realise that this is what caused his low mood. Had he realised the cause, he might have got up and gone to work and eventually the emotions stirred up by the dream would have passed. Instead, Gerald understandably assumed his depression was returning and engaged in a blizzard of negative thinking – a thought attack. That negative thinking drove his mood down even further. Understandably too, he didn't feel like getting up and he stayed in bed for too long – and staying in bed for too long leaves people feeling fatigued.

So Gerald began by experiencing one of the three components of a depression – a low mood. However, it wasn't really a component of a depression in this instance but a 'hangover' from a bad dream. Gerald then added the other two components – negative thoughts and low energy – and was in danger of sliding into an actual depression.

The lesson from Gerald's experience, and that of others, is that we should not assume that we are depressed simply because one of these components is present. When we experience low mood, negative thoughts or unexplained fatigue we need to go about our daily activities and give the symptom a chance to pass.[1]

We need strategies to help us avoid turning the blues into depression. There are three specific strategies which are linked to the triad of negative thinking, low energy and low mood: avoid brooding, maintain your energy levels and become aware of how depression 'hooks' you. After describing these I will then go on to look at a couple of other approaches which can help in dealing with depression.

TIP Never assume your depression has returned because you experience tiredness, a negative thought or a 'low' feeling. Instead take these symptoms as a signal to get busy and to stay out of the depression trap.

Brooding is bad for you!

Gerald can think for hours about the things that have gone wrong in his life, about people who have hurt him and about the ways he has let himself down. Sometimes it is after thinking in this way that Gerald begins to get depressed again. Curiously, he has never made this connection.

If you're in a hole, stop digging – that's an old and wise piece of advice, frequently ignored in many walks of life as we know! In depression, the digging is done by brooding or ruminating – going over and over the same negative thoughts and situations again and again, 'dwelling' in the negativity as it were. You can get yourself into a depression by brooding in this way – and, once in, it can be hard to get out again.

To avoid brooding yourself into a depression, it is very important, vital I would say, to interrupt yourself when you spot it happening. This isn't necessarily a matter of positive thinking, of convincing yourself that everything in the garden is rosy; sometimes positive thoughts are just too much to ask for if you're feeling really, really down. What you need to do is to gain a little distance from your thoughts. Realise they are not the be-all and end-all of everything.

It might help to understand two key things about thoughts:

1. The thoughts you are having are not necessarily true
2. Analysing your situation endlessly is usually not much help in emotional matters.

Remember Gerald? He *thinks* his depression is on the way back and that this is why he feels low – but he is wrong. He feels low because he had a disturbing dream the night before which he has forgotten about. So Gerald's thoughts are not true.

Gerald *thinks* his former lecturers and fellow students disliked him and wanted him to leave college. In fact those lecturers who knew him thought him bright and capable. Most of his fellow students were too caught up in their own concerns to pay much attention to him, especially since he made no effort to talk to them. They certainly had no desire to see him leave the college. So Gerald's thoughts about this are not true either.

This doesn't mean Gerald's thoughts are always untrue. For instance, he thinks the people at his part-time job are fed up with him for not coming to work – he's right about that. He also thinks they dislike him. That's not true: though they are annoyed at him for missing work, they actually like him as a person.

If Gerald understood that his thoughts are not necessarily true, he would see the futility of thinking endlessly about his situation. Rumination is one of the behaviours which leads people into depression. People who think on and on about a situation, who brood on it, who let the world go by as they look into their own minds, are ruminating. Endlessly analysing and ruminating on a set of untrue thoughts is simply unhelpful.

Here's an analogy: suppose you discover, after coming in from your back garden, that you no longer have your mobile phone. Suppose also that instead of going out to look for it in your back garden, where you were when it fell out of your pocket, you endlessly search the house. You're going to get nowhere. You're just going to get frustrated. That's what ruminating is like: it may lead you up and down old mental stairways and into and out of old mental rooms but it doesn't really get you anywhere useful.

One of the key insights of Buddhism is that these mental tracks we follow prevent us from seeing the real world, just as searching the house prevents us from finding the phone in the garden. So you need to put your attention outside your head. You need to get into the present. Why the present? Because when our thoughts are dragging us down *they are normally focused on another time or another place.*

'I was no good at college, they didn't like me, they all wanted me to leave' is focused on another time (the past) and another place (college). 'The people at work will be delighted when I leave' is focused on another time (the future) and another place (work). To break this vicious cycle, you need to use awareness, to focus your attention on what is going on right here and right now. Mindfulness, as described in Chapter 2, will help you to do this.

- What are the sounds and sights around you?
- Are you breathing? How do you know? Have you noticed it lately?

Awareness is a discipline. You might be surprised at how seductive your thoughts, even the painful ones, can be. But awareness of what is going on around you is a key to avoiding depression.

When you are practising awareness you will find, of course, that thoughts continue to come into your mind. Minds generate thoughts – it's what they do. But you don't have to get involved with thoughts; you can let them go on by and remain aware of the sound of the kettle boiling, music on the radio, traffic passing outside, air entering and leaving your nostrils as you breathe. In this way you can stay out of that dangerous and downward spiral into rumination.

> **TIP** When you spot yourself brooding on your troubles, stop and take yourself back gently into the here and now.

Now let's look at how you can use your physical energy to lift your mood.

Maintain energy to improve your mood
When people see Martin jogging several times a week they think he's a fitness freak. Actually, Martin detests jogging – he'd far rather sit at home and watch TV. However, he has learned that sitting at home watching TV makes him feel bad and that getting out and pushing himself a little makes him feel good. That's why he has abandoned his sofa for his runners.

The way we feel about things is influenced by the mood we are in. Our mood is influenced by our energy levels. So the way we feel about things is influenced by our energy levels.

Have you noticed how, when your energy is low, even simple tasks seem too much even though they might not require much energy to perform? Even making a telephone call can seem like climbing a mountain at such times. Yet when your energy is high, when you are 'in good form', quite difficult tasks seem very easy – even climbing a mountain seems entirely do-able!

A key fact about energy and mood is that both tend to change during the day. Generally speaking, we are likely to be in a good mood when our energy is high and in a bad mood when our energy is low. As our energy ebbs and flows, our thoughts tend to the negative or positive.

- Most people's energy peaks around mid-morning, falls to a low in the early afternoon and then rises again until about 7 p.m., when it falls until we sleep.

- Most of us are in a better, more effective mood in the morning when we seem to be able to get a lot done.
- In the early afternoon it can be very difficult to focus on what we are doing but by late afternoon we are getting into a better, more energetic mood again.

Not everyone is the same and your pattern may be different from this. Be assured, however, that you do have a pattern of rising and falling energy. This is why sleeping through the 'good' part of your day makes it so hard to get out of a depression and can leave you feeling very 'down' when you crawl out of bed.

Gerald's energy is high around mid-morning. Unfortunately, when he is feeling down, Gerald is usually still asleep at this time. Gerald gets up around half past two when his energy, and his mood, are at their lowest – no wonder he feels so awful.

His parents chide him for 'missing the best of the day'. They're right – what Gerald is missing is that part of the day when his energy and his mood are most likely to be at their highest. If he got out of bed in the morning that extra energy might lift his mood enough to begin to get him out of his depression.

Apart from being up and about in the morning, how else can you improve your mood? Well, if mood is linked to energy then one of the best ways to improve your mood is to increase your energy. And one of the most effective ways to increase your energy is to walk. Don't worry – I'm not talking about miles here! A brisk, ten-minute walk can lift your mood for an hour to an hour and a half afterwards, according to research by Dr Robert E. Thayer at California State University![2] In fact, whenever you are feeling tired during the day, a brisk walk for ten minutes will replace the tiredness with energy. Mind you, if you are prepared to walk for miles, you will get even better results. Similarly when you are in a low mood, depressed, irritable or feeling 'down', a walk can help to change that mood.

What all this means is that sometimes gloomy thoughts are just a reflection of low energy! Exactly why exercise should lift your mood is not clear, but it works. Remember, though, that most of us are put off by difficult, lengthy or demanding exercise – so pick something you enjoy. Do try it, however, when you hit a low mood or when you're tired: it's worthwhile and it costs nothing.

TIP When you're feeling down, take a good walk to lift your mood.

Become aware of how depression 'hooks' you

'You know,' Gerald's counsellor said, 'that there are benefits to depression?' 'How could there possibly be benefits to something as bad as this?' Gerald asked. 'Call them secondary benefits, payoffs, anything you like,' said the counsellor. 'These benefits can keep you depressed if you don't know about them.' Gerald got angry. 'I think that's an outrageous statement,' he complained. The counsellor grinned. 'First time I've ever seen you angry. Sure beats depression. Now, allow me to explain.'

How could something as unpleasant as depression 'hook' you? The whole notion seems ridiculous. Yet all behaviour, however ineffective, has a purpose. All behaviour is aimed at meeting one or more of your needs – though sometimes it does so in ways that carry a high price tag.

The trouble with depression is that it does a rotten job. It meets needs alright – but the price is too high and the return is too low. Dr William Glasser, who developed Reality Therapy in the early 1960s, devised the acronym ACHE to sum up the ways depression can hook any of us:

- A is for anger
- C is for control
- H is for help
- E is for excuse.

Let's see how this works.

A is for Anger

Depression is often considered an alternative to anger. If you feel bad about feeling anger towards other people, you may choose to turn that anger against yourself instead, in the form of depression. Sometimes it can even be better to choose depression than anger: if you make a habit of lashing out when anything goes wrong, you can alienate other people and make matters worse. So depression can be a safe way to react to something that goes wrong or to a loss.

Indeed if you grew up in a family in which children were not allowed to be angry, it may have been safer for you to choose depression instead. But you are no longer a child. You no longer need to deny your anger – though neither do you need to lash out. What you need is a better way of dealing with your frustrations than getting depressed. You will find some tips on how to do this in Chapter 9 (on anger) and Chapter 12 (on dealing with difficult people).

Perhaps Gerald is angry at the extent to which his parents care for him. Perhaps what he really wants to do is to tell them to get off his back. Perhaps that sort of anger is frowned upon in Gerald's home. Or maybe Gerald himself frowns upon anger to such an extent that he finds it exceptionally difficult even to feel that emotion. Depression, for these reasons, may be more acceptable to Gerald than expressing, or even feeling, his anger. However, if Gerald could firmly and fairly explain to his parents how he feels, he might not have to go through the misery of depression.

C is for Control

Depression gives you a certain amount of control over people and situations. How can it do that? Well, depression can help you to avoid taking risks. It can mean that you stay in a safe, familiar environment instead of venturing out into the world. Quite often people will try to avoid upsetting you when you are depressed.

The price for this control, however, is very high because of the suffering that comes with depression. Gerald controls his environment by staying at home and in bed. He knows he's safe there. Everything is, or seems, predictable there (though, in reality, nothing is predictable). So in that way, Gerald gets a degree of control over what's going on. It's not a type of control that's doing him any good but it is control nonetheless.

Some of the tips in Chapter 1 (on anxiety) would help Gerald get more effective control over his life.

H is for Help

Depression brings a certain amount of help. This may be help from friends, from a doctor or from an institution. Of course, we all need help from time to time. But if it goes on for too long, people may stop helping you. And in any event, depression is a high price to pay for the help you get.

Gerald gets help from his parents during his frequent bouts of depression. But wouldn't Gerald be better off standing on his own two feet?

E is for Excuse

Depression can excuse you from doing what you should do or should have done. If you are depressed, you may ask yourself, how can you be expected to get out and about, dress well, work, face your problems?

Depression gives Gerald an excuse for not going to college and for not going to work. However, it doesn't make him happy. In fact, it keeps him in pain. If he could face his anxiety, using some of the techniques in this book, he might be able to leave that pain behind him.

TIP Remember ACHE and ask yourself if depression could be trapping you in any of the ways outlined in this section.

What good is talk?

When Gerald is feeling low he prefers not to talk to anybody. It's almost as if he doesn't have the energy to talk. Quite apart from that, he cannot be bothered. He certainly does not want to have to sit there smiling and nodding and agreeing with somebody else's chatter. Neither does he want to have to listen to people telling him how easy it would be to snap out of his depression. If he could just 'snap out of it' he would have done it ages ago.

One day, however, when Gerald decides to walk to the shops, he meets a neighbour whom he sees too late to avoid. She is a pleasant person in any event, usually a cheerful sort. She chats to him for a couple of minutes about an exam her daughter has passed and which she is very pleased about and then she goes on her way. As Gerald walks on he discovers, to his surprise, that he feels much better than he has felt for days.

If you have been depressed, you know that one of the first things that happens is that people try to talk you out of it. They try to point out that things are not as bad as they seem and that if you do this or that you will feel better. They are well-meaning but, of course, it does not work. Depression is a mysterious thing which seems to rob people of the good feelings they would ordinarily get from going about their normal daily lives.

And yet, talking to people can help. A major advance in psychological research in recent years has been the discovery of mirror neurons. Neurons are networks of cells in your brain. When you think, a certain network of cells activates in your brain. If you have an angry thought one set of cells is activated; if you have a happy thought another set is activated; and if you have a depressing thought still another network is activated.

What those who have been studying mirror neurons have found is that we seem to have the ability to mirror each other when it comes to the activation of these networks of brain cells. Researchers in Europe and the United States have established that if you watch a person performing an activity such as kicking a football or drinking a cup of tea, the same networks of cells which are activated in their brains to enable these activities to happen are also activated in your brain!

If I see you being angry or sad, those cells linked to anger and sadness will activate not only in your brain but in mine as well. This is why a conversation about shopping or the weather with somebody who is reasonably cheerful can leave you feeling better. You can walk away from such a conversation feeling as though the conversation has 'taken you out of yourself'. What happens here is that the other person's positivity and cheerfulness activates similar networks of cells in your own brain. And this in turn changes your mood.

Curiously, this will very often happen when you meet somebody on the street, somebody you don't argue with out of politeness. By going along with the person in this way you allow them to influence your mood for the better. On the other hand, when your wife, your partner or a parent tells you to cheer up you are likely to argue with them and to block the effect that you could have derived from the conversation. Indeed, they may go away feeling unhappy because in your resistance and persistence you have awoken the 'depression' networks in their brains!

So if you want to put the power of mirror neurons to work for yourself, let postive people talk to you about the weather, politics or the price of cabbage. And let them bring the cheerful networks in your brain to life.

TIP Talk to positive people and notice how your mood improves.

Creating a better morning routine

Mark gets up and sits on the side of his bed. At once he thinks of remarks made to him by a colleague at work yesterday which annoyed him. How dare his colleague say such a thing?! And today he is expected to go to a meeting to argue his department's case for funding for a project which will not be well received by the other side. How unpleasant that will be! And how dare the other side take such a begrudging attitude towards his department.

It is dreary outside this morning. He can hear the rain falling on roofs and on the street. This will bring out even more cars, the traffic will be more snarled up than usual and getting to work will be a frustrating exercise.

Before long, Mark is wondering if he would be better just getting back into bed, pulling the bedclothes over his head and ignoring it all.

Is Mark alone in his self-defeating, early morning thinking? I'm afraid not! Many of us wake up and immediately begin to think of the things that went wrong yesterday or that might go wrong today. We may begin to think about things we are scared of doing but that we have to do today. Is it any wonder that by the time we get to the bathroom we are already in a dark mood? Indeed, is it any surprise that some of us do not manage to get out of bed at all? It seems so much more pleasant to stay there, snug and warm and safe, than to go out and face the dragons.

There is an alternative. It is a very simple one. This is to quite deliberately put a different set of thoughts into your head when you get up in the morning. This is best done after you have managed to get yourself out of bed and before you begin to get dressed. In other words do it during those moments when you are sitting on the bed and when your mind is beginning to generate thoughts.

What I am suggesting is that you make it a rule to think of at least four things that happened yesterday that you are pleased about. That's all there is to it, but believe me, you will sometimes have to search hard. Feeling pleased about getting a promotion or winning money on the lottery is easy. Unfortunately that does not happen every day. It may be that the best you can come up with is the fact that somebody smiled at you or that you went for a walk, but that's alright. It beats sitting there complaining about what yesterday was like or how today is going to be.

This exercise has another value too. When we are feeling blue we have a tendency to note only the negative things that have happened to us. When a person with depression tells me that nothing has changed over the past week I often find on probing that quite a number of things went well and that there were occasions when the person felt good. Somehow the memory of those positive experiences is screened out. So an exercise of this kind, which involves searching yesterday for things that went well, can help to remind you of positive events that otherwise you would simply not think of. And remembering those positive events can be of help to you in getting through the blues.

Try it out. It may seem like a small thing but it's you taking charge of your own thoughts at the start of the day and that actually is not a small thing at all.

TIP Get positive thoughts into your mind first thing in the morning – the negative thoughts can wait!

Advice from Japan
Although he felt rotten about it, Mark got up, struggled through early morning traffic and went to work. Although he had huge misgivings and fears of not being able to get the right result, he went to the meeting at which it was his job to argue for more resources for his department.

He argued back and forth. In the end, he got most of the resources he was looking for. He drove back home through still more frustrating rainy-day traffic. The sky was grey, the roads were crowded and it took half an hour longer than usual to get home. However, when he got there he found that he felt better than he had expected. That was odd, given that he had been feeling fed up all day as he went through his routine.

In Chapter 1 (on anxiety) you will find detailed information on a Japanese approach called Morita Therapy. This approach is not only usable for dealing with anxiety, it is also helpful in coping with depression and is worth looking at again here.

The approach involves three components: the first is to acknowledge the way you feel. Well, if you are depressed that is easy enough to do. Your feelings of depression loom very large. Indeed, as I mentioned in the previous section, they may loom so large that you even screen out awareness of the times when you feel well. In any event, to use this approach you begin by acknowledging how you feel.

The second part of the approach is to know what it is that you need to do. This refers to relatively simple actions. You may need to get out of bed, to pick up the telephone, to open the curtains, to make a meal or to go to the shops. There is almost always something that you need to do, so the second step is to be aware of what that is. There is no need to complicate things. The thing you need to do will usually be fairly obvious because it will usually, though not always, be a simple everyday thing.

The third part of the approach is to do that thing you need to do. Remember, you are not being asked to feel good about doing what you need to do; you are simply asked to do it regardless of whether you feel good or bad. Indeed if you are depressed you will not feel good about it until after you have done it and maybe not even then. Gradually, however, by getting things done that you need to do, you should find that your depression is shorter, that you are less influenced by your moods and that life is better.

TIP Remember, you can do the things you need to do without waiting for your mood to change.

Working with your Total Behaviour

The concept of Total Behaviour can help us to tie together, in an understandable way, much of what this chapter has discussed. The term Total Behaviour was coined by Dr William Glasser, mentioned before as the creator of Reality Therapy. At any time, four things are happening for us: what we are doing, what we are thinking, what we are feeling and what is going on in our bodies.

Sometimes these activities work in harmony. For instance, if we are pleased we may be smiling (doing), thinking positive thoughts, feeling content and physically relaxed. If we are angry we may be shouting (doing), thinking angry thoughts, feeling in a rage, with our hearts beating quickly and our muscles tensed up.

Often, the four activities are going in different directions. If you are sitting in a dentist's waiting room and you hear the drill starting up, your feelings may tell you to run but your thinking may tell you to stay. Your body may be tensed up with heart racing and adrenaline pumping – and all the while you may be thumbing idly through a dog-eared copy of *Hello!* magazine.

You could say that at all times when we are awake, and maybe even when we are asleep, we are behaving in all four ways: feeling, thinking, doing and having physical events going on. We can call this combination our Total Behaviour. A key point is this: if we can change one of the components of Total Behaviour, then we have a good chance of changing the others as well. This is because they are linked together.

But which component? It is hard to change our feelings or our physiology directly. It is easier to change what we are thinking and easiest of all to change what we are doing. So the golden rule is: if you want to change how you feel, begin by changing what you are thinking or what you are doing – especially what you are doing.

Because what you do is most in your control, you can make that speech *before* you feel confident about it; visit Aunt Eunice in the home just like you planned *even though* you feel like staying home and hoovering the house instead; get started on that assignment *even though* you *wish* you could eat a pizza and watch a DVD instead; go out to a movie *even though* you feel so comfortable sitting on that couch in front of the TV for the millionth time; have fun with your family on Saturday *even if* you feel you'd rather spend seven days a week in the office.

What does this have to do with depression? Apply the concept of Total Behaviour to depression and you get the following: what you are feeling is depressed, low, down; what you are thinking is a stream of negative thoughts about yourself, the world, the past and the future; physically you are probably low in energy; what you were doing may be anything from sitting in a chair to lying in bed, going for a walk, driving to work etc.

Of these four components, as I have mentioned before, it is what you do that you most control. In this approach East meets West: just as Morita suggested a long time ago in Japan that the way forward is to do things that need doing, Glasser suggests that when we want to change how we feel, then we need to change what we do. So if you feel lonely you may need to make a call to somebody; if you feel tired you may need to go for a brisk walk; if you feel hungry you may need to make your dinner! The key, as always, lies in what you do! Feelings follow at their own pace.

Sometimes the good feeling takes longer to arrive than we would like. If I am grieving over the end of a relationship I will, hopefully, get to the point where I am doing things I want to do – seeing friends, taking a break and so on – but it may be a long time before this 'feels' right and before I start to feel good. But if I do things I need to do, or things that matter to me, I will make that journey to feeling better much more quickly than if I immerse myself in my thoughts.

It would be wonderful to live in a world in which we always feel great about what we need to do before, during and after we do it. Many people think they live in such a world and they spend years getting nowhere as they wait for their feelings to fall into line with what they need to do. However, more often than not, the sequence is the other way around: *first* we do it, *then* we get to feel good about it.

> **TIP** If you want to change how you feel, change what you do.

Cultivate gratitude to fight the blues

Jack feels he has got nothing out of life. Others have the success, the possessions and the great relationships that he would like to have. Sometimes he sits and thinks about this for hours and gets himself into a very low mood by doing so. Jack would tell you, in all sincerity, that he has nothing to feel grateful for. But he lives in a house that his late father built and left to him; his wife earns the money that keeps the household going; and his children care about him. If Jack thought about it, he would realise that he has a great deal more to be grateful for than he now imagines. And if he was willing to cultivate gratitude, Jack would feel much better than he does right now.

Just what has gratitude got to do with ending or avoiding depression? A great deal, actually. Cultivating gratitude reduces depression in people who are already depressed, and people who cultivate gratitude are less likely to get depressed in the first place. That has been the intriguing finding in research by Dr Martin Seligman and others in the field of positive psychology. Indeed, the benefits of gratitude seem to go far beyond its role in combating depression. Generally speaking, people who feel gratitude seem to get on better in life and to be happier than those who do not.

Why should this be? Perhaps they feel better about their own experience of life; they get along better with other people and so other people get along better with them; because they feel gratitude they are more likely to do things for other people and so other people are more likely to do things for them.

Look at this from another angle: is there anybody in your life whom you think of as a bit of a miserable git? You know, stingy, complaining, never satisfied? Wouldn't it be fair to say that such a person rarely expresses gratitude? Indeed, wouldn't it be fair to say that such a person, if he cultivated gratitude, would have completely different and better relationships with the people around him?

I want to draw an important distinction here between gratitude and the feeling that you are in somebody's debt. Indebtedness is what I call the 'after all I've done for you ... ' feeling: you know, 'After all I've done for you how could you turn down that job/marry that hussy/refuse to eat your broccoli etc.' Indebtedness makes a burden out of the things another person has done for you. It is as if you have been handed a bill for past favours. We have a tendency to avoid feeling indebted and even to avoid people towards whom we feel indebted – in case they remind us.

If we fail to distinguish between gratitude and indebtedness then we may actually avoid feeling grateful because we do not want to feel indebted. But gratitude is different to indebtedness. Where indebtedness is imposed by others or by society, gratitude is freely chosen by ourselves. Gratitude occurs when I, as a free and independent human being, say yes I am grateful to you for something you did for me. Perhaps I am grateful just because you are here on this earth. It is not that I owe you gratitude, it is that I give you gratitude freely and willingly.

Indebtedness belongs to the 'after all I've done for you ... ' syndrome. Gratitude is healthy, life-giving, freely chosen and a valuable and rewarding human experience. If you are feeling depressed, you may have to dig deep to identify what you are grateful for. It may be as little as the fact that somebody made you a cup of tea yesterday or even that somebody was kind to you many years ago. Perhaps you are grateful for a favour which somebody else did for a loved one.

Although you know you are grateful for these things, you may not actually *feel* the emotion of gratitude for some time, especially if you are going through a period of depression right now. That is okay. Just know what it is that you are grateful for and let the feelings come in their own time. Give it a few weeks of finding perhaps two or three things a day that you are grateful for and let gratitude slowly begin to work its change in your life.

TIP Practice cultivating gratitude for a few weeks and see the difference it makes to how you feel.

THIS CHAPTER'S TIPS

1. Never assume your depression has returned because you experience tiredness or a negative thought or a 'low' feeling – instead take these symptoms as a signal to get busy and to stay out of the depression trap.
2. When you spot yourself brooding on your troubles, stop and take yourself back gently into the here and now.
3. When you're feeling down, take a good walk to lift your mood.
4. Remember ACHE and ask yourself if depression could be trapping you in any of the ways outlined in pages 90 to 92.
5. Talk to positive people and notice how your mood improves.
6. Get positive thoughts into your mind first thing in the morning – the negative thoughts can wait!
7. Remember, you can do the things you need to do without waiting for your mood to change.
8. If you want to change how you feel, change what you do.
9. Practice cultivating gratitude for a few weeks and see the difference it makes to how you feel.

Notes
1. Of course, if your symptom is fatigue and your daily activity involves operating machinery, brain surgery or other work requiring alertness, you should make sure you are getting enough rest and proper nutrition.
2. For more, see Dr Robert Thayer, *The Origin of Everyday Moods, Managing Energy, Tension and Stress,* Oxford University Press, 1996.

THE COUPLE'S ROAD MAP

Infatuation, conflict, resolution

7

In this chapter
- The long road
- Infatuation
- Conflict: Why can't you be more like me?
- Conflict: The battle
- Four resolutions
- Opposites attract: More on difference

The long road

In his speech at the wedding reception, Brendan's father told the usual jokes about his son's exploits as a child. Then he embarked on some fatherly advice for the couple. They had set out on a long journey, he told them. The journey would have its pleasant parts and its difficult parts, its ups and downs ... It was, to be honest, a boring speech and one that did not particularly impress Brendan and his bride Amanda. Yes, our journey will have its pleasant parts and its 'ups', they thought to themselves. But 'downs'? Difficult parts? No, no, our journey will be quite different from that of our parents, whom we have heard and seen fighting with each other from time to time. And it will be different from the journey of people we know who have ended up in the divorce courts.

And yet the stages of their journey were mapped out for them already to a greater extent than they could know. The road map would take them to a place of conflict. Where the road led after that was up to them. But they did not know this at the time.

When two people promise to stay together for life, they begin a psychological journey. The journey may differ from couple to couple but almost all couples travel through three stages: infatuation, conflict, resolution. Needless to say, this is rarely obvious at the time: that wily old saleswoman, Mother Nature, glosses over any difficulties that may lie ahead. She does this with the help of infatuation. Two people madly in love are apt to see a future together as all roses and no thorns! But thorns there will be – usually in the form of differences which emerge and sharpen and lead the partners into conflict.

Needless to say, the first reaction of most couples is to resist conflict. After all, in romantic movies and novels, their troubles end as soon as two people say *I do*. In real life, however, romance and infatuation only take them to the conflict stage, which puts their relationship to the test. That stage, conflict, can lead, though painfully, to an immeasurably stronger bond between the two people or it can kill their relationship. Alternatively, it can leave the couple existing in a permanent Cold War.

Though the examples in this chapter are of married, heterosexual couples, couples in long-term, same-sex relationships experience the same stages, passing from infatuation to resolution via the painful field of conflict.

Let's look in more detail at the three stages experienced by almost all couples as they travel their long road.

Infatuation

Brendan knows that in his life he has never met a creature as enchanting as Amanda. Her wit, her talk that seems to fill the room, her vivacity, are things Brendan has never experienced before. That a woman with such qualities wants to be with Brendan is a source of amazement and delight to him. Amanda thinks Brendan is one of the most impressive men she has ever met. He has depth – he thinks before he talks, he looks into his mind and his heart before he offers an opinion. He is comfortable with his own company. That a man like Brendan might want to be with someone like her astounds and gratifies her.

For centuries, writers have compared infatuation to a sickness! In this sickness, the sufferer sees only the perfection of their loved one. Even the ways in which they differ seem to add to the desirability of each in the other's eyes. Does she have a quick temper? Never mind – it's all part of her passionate nature and she endears herself to you every time she flies off the handle. Spend a day without her and you pine. You text her ten times a day even when you plan to meet that night. If she stayed with you forever – well, you just know you would live happily ever after.

Infatuation provides Mother Nature with her surest weapon in achieving the perpetuation of the species. As the faults of the couple vanish from each other's eyes and as their virtues magnify, the chances that these two people will get together and have babies is boosted enormously. That's why love is blind.

But infatuation ends; the glow disappears; and if all has gone to plan and the couple has produced a baby to carry the parents' genes forward, Mother Nature goes off happily, her job done.

That's the explanation from evolutionary psychology which tends to explain behaviours in terms of the perpetuation of the species. However, as I mentioned earlier, same-sex couples go through the same ecstasies and agonies as heterosexual couples: Mother Nature is an equal opportunity manipulator!

But what of our couple? Ah, now the journey gets interesting, though 'interesting' is not necessarily the word either of them would choose to describe the next stage.

TIP Enjoy infatuation – it's a wonderful experience. But when it ends, seek to deepen the relationship rather than demand the return of the heady, romantic glow.

Conflict: Why can't you be more like me?
The differences between Brendan and Amanda have become more noticeable to them both. Her witty talk has become an irritant to Brendan; his silence and introspection begin to upset Amanda.

Brendan begins to stop off at the pub for a drink on the way home from work. Amanda becomes angry at this. She sees Brendan as turning his back on her. When she complains about his late arrival home, he complains about her disappearances on Saturdays to play golf with her pals. Brendan happens to be one of those people who cannot see any point to golf. He has no interest whatsoever in listening to Amanda going on about it or, perish the thought, in playing golf with her as she has suggested.

A million other little differences arise: she likes to sleep with the lights on, which he regards as monstrously inconsiderate. He likes to dress in sloppy clothes and go around unshaven on his days off; she can't stand untidiness.

Differences between the couple begin to emerge in the first part of the conflict stage. What had amused now begins to grate on the nerves. The reality of living with another person day in and day out strikes home. Each person feels a little intolerant of some aspects of the other person's behaviour. Each reads meanings into the other's behaviour. If you loved me, one says, you would not want to spend time in the pub with your friends. If you loved me, the other replies, you would not criticise me the way you do.

Remember, the details differ from couple to couple. Differences in behaviour may matter more to one partner than to the other; or one may criticise or defend more than the other. However, those first stirrings of discontent can, and often do, lead to a second stage of sharper conflict.

TIP Annoying differences don't necessarily mean there is anything flawed about either of you – they simply mean you are different people with different preferences.

Conflict: The battle

Brendan and Amanda now fight every week. Their fights can last for days. Not that they shout or scream at each other for days – the actual argument is over very quickly, but then the silence kicks in. That silence goes on for days at a time and is upsetting and exhausting for them both.

The things that set off their arguments tend to be very small: a glance, a particular tone of voice, one or the other of them being a few minutes late getting home, Brendan leaving his socks on the floor or Amanda putting his Sunday paper in the recycle bin before he has finished reading it.

The triviality of the issues about which they fight often embarrasses couples who come to marriage counselling. However, almost all rows between couples are about minor matters, the small change of everyday life. The underlying state of conflict turns spats into rows.

In other chapters we will explore some of the ways people fight, ways which, in the long run, make matters worse. Generally speaking, as a couple you will fight if you are human – how you fight and the assumptions you bring to your conflicts will go a long way towards determining the future of your relationship.

In this chapter I map out the stages most long-term relationships pass through. A knowledge of these stages will, in itself, help enormously. The realisation that your situation mirrors that of other couples can help you bring a degree of understanding and even tolerance to your conflicted relationship.

In the conflict stage, each partner says to the other: I want you to be more like me. And behind that they ask: What's wrong with you? Eventually, the conflict stage usually, and fortunately, draws to a close. Resolution follows – happy or unhappy. Let's look at four of the many possible outcomes which characterise resolution.

TIP Beware of demanding that your partner be more like you – such demands could threaten your relationship.

Four resolutions

Outcome 1: Ending the relationship

On the day they signed the separation agreement, Brendan found himself wondering how it had ever come to this. Then he reminded himself quickly of what an utterly unreasonable person Amanda was. Amanda, too, wondered how it had come to this and she too reminded herself quickly what an unreasonable person Brendan was. Neither voiced this opinion to the other. They had reached the point at which they would communicate only through their solicitors. The disintegration of their marriage had started with small disagreements and, Brendan realised with a jolt, had continued with small disagreements all the way to this day. Dropping a plate on the floor, running out of petrol, forgetting to pay the phone bill or coming home late in an evening hardly seemed to merit a week or two of pained silence. Yet both had engaged in this behaviour. Finally, it had seemed best for them and for the children that they part – though they had not actually asked the children for their opinion. In a way, he reflected, separation was not what he and Amanda wanted. And yet, they could not live together. Another month together would drive him insane. And Amanda, sitting in her solicitor's office, was thinking the same.

Locked into a pattern of escalating conflict, partners begin to see each other in an entirely negative light. They lose their capacity to speak to each other even for a few minutes without a fight. At an extreme, marriage counselling provides an opportunity for yet another row, this time in front of the counsellor. And since every conversation leads to a row, they can no longer even talk about how to save the relationship.

Outcome 2: Developing mutual tolerance

Brendan has never been terribly good at saying how he feels or what he wants. This used to drive Amanda crazy. 'How the hell am I supposed to know what is going on in your mind if you won't tell me?' she used to say. But now she accepts that this is the way Brendan is. Like a bloody cryptic crossword, she laughs. Brendan used to get really annoyed because Amanda was so critical. He would sulk for days sometimes because she had made a criticism of him. In time, though, he came to see that this was simply her way. Can't keep her opinion to herself whether or not it's worth giving away, he laughs. But Brendan and Amanda get along well together; they have fun and they love each other. And they have learned to tolerate each other's shortcomings.

Many couples end the conflict stage with a (usually!) good humoured tolerance of each other's foibles and of what they see as each other's faults. Their love, they realise, matters more than their differences. They learn to joke about these differences. This outcome makes space for love and laughter and for a good and fulfilling relationship between two people. It provides their children with an example of how to get along with other people. It ranks as one of the good outcomes.

Outcome 3: Cold War

Every evening, when he comes home from work, Brendan goes straight to the sitting-room, pours himself a drink and switches on the television. If Amanda has not heard him coming in the front door, she knows he is home when she hears the television starting up. She heats up his dinner in the microwave then puts it on the table, goes to the sitting-room door, sticks her head in and says it's ready. Then she goes upstairs to her bedroom and Brendan eats his dinner alone in the kitchen.

When he has eaten, Brendan will return to the sitting-room and commence watching television again. Amanda will come down and watch television in the kitchen. Amanda will go to bed at 1 a.m. Brendan will already be asleep. In the whole day they will have exchanged no more than a dozen words. This will go on for another twenty-five years.

The Cold War outcome brings years of dull pain. The partners fight relatively little compared to before but their disapproval of each other freezes the atmosphere. Each lives with their face turned away from the other. They have little to say to each other and what they do have to say involves minimal conversations about such issues as housekeeping and child rearing. Expressions of love have long disappeared. Love itself perhaps has long disappeared. They stay together out of fear of the wider world or for the sake of the children. These reasons for staying together have their own validity – but who would welcome a life like this?

Outcome 4: Creative acceptance

Brendan reckons Amanda has gone a little bit daft. So far as he can see, she is always chasing the latest fad from India or California. But Brendan loves Amanda and has to admit to himself that life would be dull if she were not the way she is. Amanda, on the other hand, tells him he is a typical accountant and that he feels at home only with a spreadsheet. She is joking, but not too much. She has grown to like his seriousness and to get fun out of teasing him about it. He makes sure to be home to mind the kids if she wants to go off on a spiritual weekend or whatever the latest thing may be. And she makes sure to be at home when he goes to a meeting of the Organisation of Chartered Treasurers of which he is chairman. They still make the effort to go out together and they take one holiday a year alone without the children. Neither would really want the other to be any way but the way that they are.

Creative acceptance brings not only a toleration of each other's differences but also support for the other on that person's journey through life. Each may take on new interests and try new things with the other's support, or may develop existing interests. The couple still fight now and then but they end their fights more quickly than before. They avoid the silences that follow fights or they break these silences more quickly.

These four outcomes, and many possible others, emerge from relationship conflict.[1] Conflict and long-term human relationships go together. What matters is learning to handle everyday conflict with tolerance and humour. This is not to say that every conflict can be overcome. An affair or violence for instance can destroy a marriage no matter how much one or both of the partners want it to survive. Nevertheless, by dealing with everyday conflict wisely and tolerantly couples can greatly increase the chances that their relationship will survive their differences and will even be enhanced by them.

TIP The conflict stage can end in one of many ways. Here are four common outcomes: the breakup of the relationship; mutual tolerance; Cold War; or creative acceptance of each other. Which do you want and what will you do to get it?

Opposites attract: More on difference

People still wonder what Manus and Catherine see in each other. Manus does not seem to do very much, that anyone can see. True he goes out to work every day in a hardware store but you could not by any stretch of the imagination describe him as the most dynamic businessman in town. Indeed he is apt to close the store to go across the street for a drink or to go to the races when they are on locally. Catherine, on the other hand, has at least three businesses running at the same time: a farm, a driving school and a boutique in the town. She is up and bustling about long before Manus awakes. You could not imagine a more unsuitable partner for her than Manus. And yet, and this is what really puzzles people, Manus and Catherine are happy.

Opposites attract. It happens uncannily often that people fall head over heels in love with those who differ from them psychologically, emotionally or in terms of their social behaviour. These differences, far from putting people off, seem to enhance the attraction. A party animal falls for a person who prefers to spend time on her own; a thrifty person finds herself dazzled by a dashing guy who throws caution to the winds and whose credit card groans under the weight of debt.

Why opposites attract in this way has long sparked debate. Perhaps each completes the other: you have what I do not have; I have what you do not have; bring us together and you have someone who is more complete than either of us on our own. Or perhaps we evolved to attract our opposites: children who experience very different parents learn skills which will help them deal with the variety of people who await them on their path through life.

However, opposites don't just attract – later they repel! The party animal comes to seem frivolous to the solitary person. In turn, her ability to spend lots of time with herself, once so admirable, may now seem boring. The big spender threatens the family finances – or so it appears to the thrifty one, and in turn the thrifty one strikes the carefree spender as a spoilsport.

This switch, from opposites that attract to opposites that repel, throws couples into the conflict stage. It accounts for a good deal of the pain that accompanies the maturing of relationships. But when you know that this switch happens for many, many couples and not just for you, your chances of negotiating conflict successfully improve immediately.

If only things were arranged differently and couples could skip this stage of conflict! But whether we like it or not, the conflict stage waits in the wings for almost every couple as they walk up the aisle on their big day.

I said earlier that each couple's conflict has its own peculiarities, its own specific issues and its own characteristics. These often arise from conditions that existed before the couple met. In the next chapter we take a look at these conditions. If you can recognise them in yourself, then you can start to negotiate your relationship out of conflict and into a far better place.

TIP The things that annoy you about each other may be what attracted you in the first place – so maybe a little tolerance and acceptance is in order!

THIS CHAPTER'S TIPS

1. Enjoy infatuation – it's a wonderful experience. But when it ends, seek to deepen the relationship rather than demand the return of the heady, romantic glow.
2. Annoying differences don't necessarily mean there is anything flawed about either of you – they simply mean you are different people with different preferences.
3. Beware of demanding that your partner be more like you – such demands could threaten your relationship.
4. The conflict stage can end in one of many ways. Here are four common outcomes: the breakup of the relationship; mutual tolerance; Cold War; or creative acceptance of each other. Which do you want and what will you do to get it?
5. The things that annoy you about each other may be what attracted you in the first place – so maybe a little tolerance and acceptance is in order!

Note

1. This process is described well in *The Couple's Journey* by Susan M. Campbell, PhD, Impact Publishers, 1980.

LONG-TERM RELATIONSHIPS

Lessons from the battlefield

8

In this chapter
- Conflict in marriage: Three key points
- The question of control
- Two bad thinking habits
- Basic Naikan exercise
- The insistence on being right
- I didn't mean it! Yes you did!

Conflict in marriage: Three key points
'I don't know what's wrong with Stanley and your Martha,' said Stanley's uncle. 'They had a big fight on their holiday. Why can't they be more like my favourite nephew John and his lovely wife Marie who never fight?'
'Oh, that reminds me,' said Martha's mother with a sweet smile. 'Did I tell you John and Marie are getting divorced?'

In looking at conflict in a long-term relationship, there are three key points to bear in mind. If you take these points to heart, you will handle conflict better and you will have a better relationship with your partner.

The first key point is that couples fight. In the beginning, when two people are infatuated and 'mad about' each other they can find it hard to believe that a day will come when they will be seriously 'mad at' each other. Of course, many couples understand that rows are part of any long-term relationship. It is just as well that they understand this: research shows that couples who believe that fighting has no place in a loving relationship are at particularly high risk of break-up. It is not hard to see why. Couples with this belief have two hurdles to get over after they have a row: first, they have to get over or get beyond whatever the issue was they were fighting about; second, they have to get over the fact that they had a row in the first place.

With this amount of 'getting over' to be done, it takes longer to restore harmony. Rows that drag on forever and a day, usually in the form of offended silences, are the enemies of long-term relationships. So accepting that fights happen in even the best of relationships is the first step towards dealing with them in as sensible a way as possible. This is not to say that there are any especially sensible ways to fight – but there are better ways and worse ways and which way you choose can make all the difference.

The second key point is that most of the issues you fight over in your relationship will probably remain unresolved. Research in the United States by John Gottman and his wife Julie came up with the surprising finding that even in successful, long-term relationships most of the issues on which the couple disagree remain unresolved.

What this suggests is that to demand that another person change their ways completely is probably a waste of time and nothing more than a source of aggravation. Human beings differ so much in their preferences and in their experiences that complete agreement, even between the members of a loving couple, is impossible to achieve. Clearly a partner, male or female, whose attitude is 'my way or the highway' is condemning the couple to fight after fruitless fight, a situation which may destroy the relationship. Understanding that most issues remain unresolved enables us to take a more realistic and tolerant view of each other.

By putting these two facts together – that all couples fight from time to time and that most of the issues remain unresolved – we come to the third key point. What really matters about conflict in the long-term relationship is the way it is handled.

Many a marriage counsellor will wearily tell you that what couples embarking on a lifetime together most need to be able to do is to learn how to fight. What they mean is that couples need to learn how to fight well as opposed to how to fight stupidly. Admittedly marriage counsellors are somewhat biased in this regard. They see couples at their worst and all too often at the stage when therapy cannot succeed because the couple are incapable of having a conversation with each other, even in the presence of a stranger. And while the issues are sometimes not all that complex in themselves, very often the way they fight over them escalates the conflict into something that can wreck the marriage.

It is in the spirit of these three points, and in the light of their implications, that the remainder of this chapter is written.

TIP Bear in mind that though couples have rows, most of the issues between them are never fully resolved – even in successful relationships.

The question of control

Bill liked a tidy desk, a tidy house, a tidy car and a tidy wife. Unfortunately, Becky saw tidiness as a waste of life's best years. Bill and Becky fought a lot about this.

Becky liked a husband who would go shopping with her on Saturdays and relax and read the newspaper with her on Sundays. That was what her father did and that was what Bill must do. Bill refused to go shopping and insisted on playing golf on Sundays. Bill and Becky fought a lot about this.

It is probable that the greatest marriage conflicts arise out of attempts by one partner to control the other or even by both partners to control each other. Human beings tend to resist attempts by others to control them. This is the sort of thing we all know but blithely ignore when it comes to our loved ones. Even where one partner allows themselves to be controlled, time often brings a change of heart, the worm turns and the partner leaves the relationship.

The general rule, then, is that if either partner makes control a key issue, conflict is likely to be continuous and possibly terminal. If you look at your role in conflict in your relationship – and this applies to men and women – you will almost certainly find that the desire to control the other person's behaviour, or to control the situation, is a factor.

This doesn't make you a control freak. As human beings we have evolved to control ourselves, people and situations to meet our needs and to get what we want. In fact, controlling our behaviour is so natural to us that we do it without thinking. To take a simple example mentioned earlier: I stroll to the shop daydreaming and unaware of my surroundings, yet I usually end up where I want to go: I am able to control my direction and my walking even though I am not really aware of what I am doing!

Or take a somewhat more scary example: have you ever driven from one place to another without any memory of the journey? So innate has control become that you actually drove the car, and survived, though you were a million miles away in your head. On safety grounds, I do not recommend this as a normal way of doing things!

We have evolved to seek enough control to meet our basic needs. The most important word to notice here is 'we' because 'we' includes everybody. You need a certain amount of control; your partner needs a certain amount of control. The boss needs a certain amount of control – but so does the worker. The parent needs a certain amount of control – but so does the child. The customer needs a certain amount of control – but so does the shopkeeper.

When people fail to recognise that the other person also has a need for control, the stage is set for conflict. This is because a failure to recognise the other person's need for control is generally accompanied by a refusal to negotiate and compromise. And believe me, if you want to have a long-term relationship with another human being you had better be able to negotiate and compromise.

When we fail to recognise that each of us has a legitimate need for control we tend to see only our own side of the story and to denigrate the other person's point of view. Instead of asking we demand; instead of seeking a joint way we insist on our own way.

At the other extreme, we may fail to see that our own desire for control is legitimate. In such a case we are in danger of allowing ourselves to be walked on. We may retreat into seeking a false sense of control such as by drinking.

Control is all around us, in both effective and ineffective ways. If I'm scared to go to work and I stay in bed instead, I am trying to control my situation at least to the extent of not going to work. If I go to my union, my boss or my doctor about my fears I am also trying to control my situation, perhaps more effectively.

If I buy a lottery ticket I am trying to exercise a little bit of control over my future, however poor the chances of winning. If I pay into a pension scheme I am also trying to control my future.

If I hear there's going to be a petrol shortage and I hoard petrol, I am trying to gain a little control over the future. If I buy a bicycle or check out bus and train times I am also trying to control the future to cope with the petrol shortage.

If I boss people around I am trying to get control over them. And if they find a way to cheat me or con me they are trying to get some of their control back.

In marriage, ineffective attempts at controlling include criticising, sulking, long silences, doors slammed or walking out of the house. In fact, attempts to control other persons are almost always ineffective. We have little enough control over our own thoughts – try to think of nothing for one minute and you'll see! – and hardly any direct control over our feelings. How then can we realistically expect to have control over another person?

One person may go along with what another wants for the sake of peace, out of fear or because they value the relationship above their own individual autonomy. However, there is a good chance that even persons who are quite cowed by a partner will kick against that control eventually. This is because their basic human need for their own control and autonomy will not allow them to write themselves out of their own life story in the way that the control freak wants them to.

Most of us, luckily, have no interest in exercising that degree of control over somebody else. Yet if you learn to observe your behaviour you will see that we are all prone to trying to control our environment – and our environment, after all, includes other people.

In a long-term relationship what we need to aim for is not to control another person but to exercise control alongside that other person. This takes a capacity for negotiation and compromise. So if your relationship is heading for the rocks, check whether it might be affected by futile control battles and see whether these battles can be replaced with a compromise that gets each of you enough of what you want.

TIP Watch out for the human tendency, on both your parts, to try to control the other person. Aim for joint control.

Two bad thinking habits

Michael was twenty minutes late for his date with Margaret. He has decided that it's ok now to keep me waiting, she told herself. He'd rather make another call at work than get himself here at the right time. By the time he arrived, she was angry and she snapped at him. Michael had been held up in traffic delayed by an accident on the way to meet Margaret. He had really been looking forward to their evening together. When he explained, Margaret cheered up and did her best to make up for her earlier complaint. But for Michael their date was ruined: Margaret's attitude when they met had soured it and he sulked through the rest of the evening. Margaret and Michael have been the victims of mind-reading and of all-or-nothing thinking.

Two thinking habits in particular are enemies of relationships. These are mind-reading and all-or-nothing thinking.

Mind-reading

I have referred elsewhere to how mind-reading – imagining that you know what other people are thinking – increases anxiety. But mind-reading also creates unnecessary and unjustified anger and resentment in relationships.

- 'I'm sure she thinks I'm terrible'
- 'He couldn't care less about how I feel'
- 'She says she loves me but I know she's just making the best of a bad lot.'

These are all examples of mind-reading.

Your partner gets up and walks out of the room. You assume she is angry with you, so now you get angry with her – all on the basis of mind-reading. Perhaps she got up and walked out of the room because she suddenly remembered something that she needed to do. If so, your anger is based on a fiction created by you. Indeed, when you find yourself the target of resentment and silences it may well be that you are the unwitting victim of mind-reading on the part of your partner. The wise thing would be to ask her what it is that she is upset about – though at times many of us, I am afraid, would rather not know!

Watch out for the harmful effects of mind-reading on your relationship. Remind yourself that in reality there is no such thing as mind-reading – there is only guesswork. If you want to find out what somebody is thinking, you will just have to ask!

All-or-nothing thinking

We are probably at our most immature when we engage in all-or-nothing thinking. When we think in this way we see things as either all right or all wrong.

- 'He's a complete jerk'
- 'She lied to me once. I can never trust her again'
- 'If he's five minutes late he couldn't possibly care about me.'

These are examples of all-or-nothing thinking.

All-or-nothing thinking usually accompanies anger: suddenly the other person is the worst in the world and all the good that they have done is forgotten. Actually, it doesn't matter very much that we think in this silly way when we're angry so long as we get over it quickly enough. However, it matters very much indeed if we begin to apply all-or-nothing thinking to our partner as a matter of course. All-or-nothing thinking is always a lie. It never, ever tells the whole truth about the other person. I cannot imagine a long-term relationship that can flourish in any healthy way when one or both partners are determined to engage in this kind of thinking.

Each person in the relationship, after all, will inevitably get things wrong, will inevitably do things that offend the other person and will inevitably be a complete pain in the neck now and then. However, each person will also have done many things for the other, will have engaged in loving behaviours and will perhaps have put up with a certain amount of bad behaviour coming from the other direction. It is when this positive side is forgotten that all-or-nothing thinking does most harm.

TIP When you spot yourself mind-reading or doing all-or-nothing thinking, remind yourself that these mental habits are the enemies of good relationships.

It is vital to watch out for this kind of thinking and to challenge it in yourself. Here is an exercise that can help. It's a Japanese exercise called Naikan. Try it and you will be surprised at how quickly Naikan can get you out of all-or-nothing thinking.[1]

Basic Naikan exercise
Ask yourself these questions. You can take as short or as long a time over them as you wish.

First question
What have I received from this person? The question refers to positive actions the person has performed for you. Be specific in your answers. Answers can range all the way from having your children to making your dinner most nights (and if you are like most of us, your wife does most of the cooking and washing and tidying whatever your good intentions might be). Maybe she makes sure you get out of bed in the morning in time to get to work; maybe she reminds you about your mother's birthday; maybe she does the driving when you both go out to the pub. If you have to dig for the answers, then dig for them.

Second question
What has this person received from me? Again, look for positive actions you have performed for her. Maybe you have been her partner in rearing of children; maybe you bring her up a cup of tea in bed every morning; maybe you buy her a gift now and then; maybe your income meets most of the household bills; maybe you brought her car for its NCT test.

Third question
What troubles have I caused this person? Maybe you are consistently late when you both meet in town; maybe you don't wash up after you have a snack; maybe you leave her to do most of the housework; maybe she is the one who always has to drive when you both go for a drink; maybe you have ignored her requests not to leave your clothes on the floor; maybe you sulk when you don't get your way.

Fourth question
Aha! There is no fourth question!

If this exercise was symmetrical we all know what the fourth question would be – but we don't ask it in this exercise because you probably already spend too much time and energy chewing on the things your partner does to annoy you. You really don't need to do an exercise to be reminded of them!

What you need to be reminded of are the answers to the first three questions. This does not mean that you are encouraged to beat yourself up. All the exercise does is bring some balance into your thinking about your partner. When a relationship goes wrong, that balance disappears very quickly. Sometimes it is only when the relationship is over that the good side of it, or what you could have done differently, is recalled. Why not recall these things now?

The Naikan exercise can be used in any conflict situation with colleagues, customers, the company that employs you and so on.

> **TIP** When you're really fed up with your partner, try a little Naikan and see what happens.

The insistence on being right
Simon and Carol were each convinced that they were absolutely right about everything. This created endless rows when they disagreed and their rows never got them anywhere: after all, if both were right and they disagreed, both must be wrong. They fought over the right time to get up, the right way to go to work, how to discipline the children, how often to visit his mother, how often to visit her mother and on and on and on. They were exhausted and they were not happy but they both grew up in families dominated by a parent who insisted on being right all the time so they knew no other way.

In Chapter 4, I have outlined how we disturb our own peace of mind by an insistence on always being right in the various situations in which we find ourselves. This insistence is particularly bad for our close relationships. Indeed, I would go so far as to say that the insistence on being right is the enemy of peace. On the other hand, being willing to allow your partner to influence you and the relationship can deepen the experience for both of you. Dr Abraham Low, who founded Recovery Inc in Chicago in the 1930s, believed that the insistence by family members on being right actually drove other family members mad! Certainly it does little good for any long-term relationship.

The partner who insists on being right about everything will fight about anything:

- What colour paper should be on the wall? Only this one!
- What movie should we go to? Only this one!
- What school should the children go to? Only this one!
- Which shirt should I wear? Only this one!
- What time should you be in from a night out? At this time and no later!
- What channel should we watch on the television? Only this one!
- Should we walk on the footpath or on the grass? Whichever I say!

The list is truly endless. People who insist on being right all the time anger and dominate other people and are often angry and bitter themselves. What makes them angry and bitter is the fact that they live in a world which will not live up to their expectations. They are continually frustrated by their partners, their children, the government, the weather, the transport system and a myriad of other forces that will not dance to their tune.

If you are a person who insists on being right then I would urge you to consider the benefits of allowing others to be right for a change. Even if you secretly think yourself to be right all the time consider the benefits of keeping that opinion to yourself on, let's say, 50 per cent of the occasions that your partner is, in your view, doing or saying the wrong thing.

Remember, most of the things that people insist on being right about don't actually matter. Can you remember all the things you were insisting on being right about this day last year? No. That insistence on being right may be linked to some childhood shame or it may simply be a style of relating that you picked up from somebody else. Either way, the insistence on being right all the time is not worth the trouble it creates in relationships.

And if it is the other person in the relationship who insists on being right, all I can suggest is that you show them this section of the book!

TIP Beware of exhausting yourself and everyone else by insisting on being right every time – allow yourself the luxury of being wrong and see the difference it makes.

I didn't mean it! Yes you did!

Frank is untidy: he leaves socks and shirts on the floor and this really angers Mary, not just because she has asked him a million times to stop doing it but because she reckons he does it to annoy her. On Saturdays when Frank wants to get out to play golf he's often held up because Mary takes a long time to get back from the supermarket with the weekly shopping and she has left him in charge of the kids. This really angers John because he reckons she takes her time just to get at him.

Needless to say, anger is a familiar visitor to most long-term relationships! This is inevitable. However, there are ways to stop anger from getting out of hand and destroying the relationship.

First, separate anger from intention. In Chapter 4, I pointed out the fallacy of assuming that what annoys us in other people's behaviour is intended by them to be annoying. Most annoyances are unintended – they are simply an unplanned by-product of people's actions. Recognising this fact is a key sign of maturity in intimate relationships.

This principle is so important that it is worth looking at again in the context of relationship conflict.

Here are some behaviours that can be annoying – and may need to be addressed – but that are rarely if ever intended as such:

- Being late for a date
- Forgetting an anniversary
- Not tidying up
- Hogging the phone
- Leaving the toilet seat up
- Snoring
- Going out with friends instead of staying home with your partner
- Having friends or relatives in the house every day.

As members of Recovery Inc tell themselves when they start getting angry: people do things *that* annoy me not *to* annoy me. This is a marvellous affirmation and if you learn it and use it you will save yourself a lot of trouble. The fact is, we get far more angry when we think people are deliberately setting out to annoy us than we do when something happens that is merely annoying in itself.

In a long-term relationship it is crucial to distinguish between those things your partner does which are intentionally annoying and those which are not. By and large, when your spouse annoys you the annoyance is generated by you and not by her. Yes, it's annoying if she insists on acting as a navigator when you're driving – but getting you angry is not usually the purpose of this behaviour. It may simply be a learned behaviour or a matter of thoughtlessness or of nervousness.

During such times, and especially if there is tension between you, it is invaluable to remind yourself that people do things *that* annoy you, not *to* annoy you.

Watch out for angry thinking, too, to avoid doing unnecessary harm to a relationship. Angry thoughts produce angry outbursts.

Marcus is on his way home from work. He's a little late. He had an argument with Sheila last night and he's chewing it over in his mind. He gets angrier and angrier as he dwells on the things that were said. No doubt she's angry too and she'll nag at him for being late as soon as he gets through the door. By the time he gets home he's really stewing and he snaps at her before he has time to see her welcoming smile. The evening is ruined – again.

Tomorrow morning she will snap at him when he slams the door of the dishwasher – but it will really be because a news story about political greed and incompetence has started her thinking angry thoughts. But Marcus doesn't realise this so he stalks off to work in a temper.

And so it goes on. Angry thinking makes for fights that never need to happen. When you spot it, step out of that angry fantasy and into the here and now – notice the sights and sounds around you, notice your own breathing. Get out of your head and into the real world and save yourself and your loved ones a lot of trouble.

There is more on anger in Chapter 9.

TIP Learn this thought and repeat it often: People do things *that* annoy me not *to* annoy me.

THIS CHAPTER'S TIPS

1. Bear in mind that though couples have rows, most of the issues between them are never fully resolved – even in successful relationships.
2. Watch out for the human tendency, on both your parts, to try to control the other person. Aim for joint control.
3. When you spot yourself mind-reading or doing all-or-nothing thinking, remind yourself that these mental habits are the enemies of good relationships.
4. When you're really fed up with your partner, try a little Naikan and see what happens.
5. Beware of exhausting yourself and everyone else by insisting on being right every time – allow yourself the luxury of being wrong and see the difference it makes.
6. Learn this thought and repeat it often: people do things *that* annoy me not *to* annoy me.

Note

1. Naikan was brought to the West by David Reynolds as part of his Constructive Living approach.

ANGER

Tips for angry people

9

In this chapter

- Avoid feeding yourself angry thoughts
- Describe your feelings instead of acting them out
- Try to control less, not more
- Feel the anger physically, not in your head
- Stop before you get to the top of the stairs

Most of us feel angry every day over something. It may be about the weather, the government, a late delivery or any of a host of other frustrations. Usually, the anger rises, falls and is gone. For some of us, however, the anger we feel at these and other events is sharper and lasts for longer. It can even be catastrophic, as mirrored by newspaper reports of serious assaults arising out of the most minor frustrations. Even those of us who do not have an 'anger problem' can be surprised and distressed when we find ourselves exploding in anger in certain situations. In the long term, excessive anger damages relationships and results in actions which the angry person may later bitterly regret.

The tips in this chapter will help you to keep anger in its place. You will also find earlier material on mind-reading[1] helpful, as assuming people are thinking bad things about you can fuel your anger. Be sure also to read what I wrote earlier on the mistake of assuming deliberate intent on the part of people whose behaviour annoys you.[2]

Avoid feeding yourself angry thoughts

Andrew snapped at his daughter when she tapped him on the arm to ask for money for a school trip. The child ran out of the room, distressed and in tears. Andrew himself was surprised and distressed by his own behaviour. What had gone wrong? Just before his daughter interrupted

129

him, Andrew had been listening to a news item about government plans to double parking fees. For Andrew, this would mean a big extra cost, and he had been thinking angrily about how government ministers don't have to bother with parking or parking fees because they've all got their official drivers, paid for by people like Andrew. He was also thinking about how helpless people like him were to stop things like this from happening. So when his daughter tapped him on the arm, Andrew was already angry and she was the lightning conductor through which his anger was channelled.

Drivers involved in road-rage incidents usually turn out to have been angry when they got into the car to begin their journey. As they drove along they had been feeding themselves with angry thoughts about some frustration or other and when an unfortunate person crossed their path they were ready to let fly – and they did.

This does not just apply to road-rage incidents. If you think back to occasions on which you over-reacted and flew off the handle you will probably find that you had been thinking some very angry thoughts before the incident happened. Sometimes these thoughts were related to the incident but very often they had nothing to do with it at all. So when you find yourself chewing over angry thoughts, simply take your attention away from these thoughts and back to whatever is going on around you. Using the mindfulness approach described in Chapter 2 will help you do this.

TIP Always interrupt angry thoughts as soon as you spot them.

Describe your feelings instead of acting them out

Tony was twenty-two but still behaved like a two-year-old. He expected his mother to look after him, to feed and clothe him, and to anticipate his needs. He did not work because he had not yet come across a job that was worthy of his talents. If Tony did not like the food his mother prepared or if, say, she refused to spend yet more money on his clothes, he would shout, break things and sometimes hit her. Tony's mother eventually got sense and took out a barring order against him. Tony moved in with friends but after he threw his first tantrum, they threw him out. Life is beginning to look uncomfortable for Tony.

Acting out your feelings means letting rip, letting go, letting it all out with no regard for other people. In the case of anger it can mean shouting, screaming, saying the most hurtful things you can think of, pushing, hitting, breaking, throwing, even hurting yourself in front of someone else.

Describing your feelings, on the other hand, means telling people how you feel, trying to explain it to them, trying to make people understand. 'I'm angry with you for coming home late. I felt so worried about you' – this is describing your feelings and it's a lot less damaging than screaming at your teenage daughter when she walks in the door, pushing her or flinging her dinner against the wall.

Describing your feelings allows you to communicate how you feel without indulging in damaging behaviours and is almost always better than acting out your anger.

TIP Instead of acting out your anger, simply describe what it is that you are angry about. In both the long and the short run, this approach is far more likely to get you the cooperation of other people.

Try to control less, not more
Now in his seventies, Greg has been getting angry for decades at the choices his children make – and he's let them know it, too. Everything from their choice of career, to their choice of partner, to where they choose to live, to the schools they send his grandchildren to can really frustrate Greg if he

disapproves. When they were children, they toed the line but they have long since given up letting Greg dictate to them. Greg, however, is used to controlling the situations in which he finds himself and he is not about to give up the habit of a lifetime. As a result, he sees very little of his children and grandchildren.

Trying to control too much of what goes on around you leads to frustration and anger. Other people's behaviour, thoughts and feelings are outside your control and trying to control them can make you get mad very fast! One of the basic needs we all have is for autonomy and the freedom to make our own choices. For that reason, the control freak never receives unquestioning obedience and is therefore in a constant state of frustration. The mixture of control and resistance makes for unhappy relationships and can leave long-term emotional scars.

You can, of course, try to influence other people and ask them to do certain things. You can even use your powers of persuasion on other people, often with success. Whether they comply with what you want is in their control, not yours. So, as much as possible, focus on your own behaviour instead of frustrating yourself over the behaviour of other people.

TIP Try to influence other people by all means, but drop the illusion that you can control their behaviour.

Feel the anger physically, not in your head

When Dermot gets angry he starts off a monologue in his mind in which he heartily curses and denounces whoever it is that has upset him. Sometimes, he starts up this monologue when he sees somebody coming, say at work, who has made him angry in the past. After a few seconds of this, Dermot is angry all over again. When Dermot is sent by his employer to anger management classes, he is told to stay out of his head and instead note the physical symptoms that accompany his anger. When he starts doing this, Dermot, to his own surprise, gets angry less often and when he does get angry he can keep this anger under control.

When you feel angry your attention is, naturally enough, directed towards whatever it is that is making you angry. Switching your attention onto something else can greatly reduce the anger you feel and, perhaps more importantly, can prevent your anger from escalating to the point at which you do something you later regret. That switching of attention is easier said than done, of course. What is normally do-able, though, is to focus your attention on the physical symptoms that go along with your anger.

So instead of getting caught up in thinking about whatever you're angry about, notice how the anger feels physically. How is it affecting your chest, your stomach, your head for instance? Do you get physically hot when you're angry? Can you feel your heart beating faster? Does your face feel flushed? Focusing on your physical sensations in this way takes your attention away from the event or thought that you are angry about and puts it on to your own physical reactions instead. If you stay with noticing your physical reactions, your anger will begin to subside.

TIP Prevent the escalation of anger by putting your attention on your physical experience.

Stop before you get to the top of the stairs

Michael's problem is not that he gets angry. The problem is that he can so quickly go from the first stirrings of anger to shouting, waving his arms about, saying terribly abusive things and punching the walls and doors. Michael learned this from his mother, who had learned it from her father.

When he gets a chance to stand back and look at his behaviour in counselling, Michael sees how ridiculous it is and how destructive it can be. In addition to some of the other anger management techniques in this chapter, Michael learns the 'top of the stairs' technique and finds it works for him straight away.

Imagine a stairs leading from the ground floor to the top floor of a house. Imagine that when you are on the ground floor you feel calm as you go about your daily business. Imagine also that when you are at the top of the stairs you are in an absolute rage – shouting, stamping about, throwing things, hitting things, hurting people. As you rush up that stairs, you get angrier and angrier. Sometimes you rush right to the top in a matter of seconds!

What you need to do is to learn to stop when you spot yourself climbing that stairs. Tell yourself to stay on the lower steps. Down on the lower steps you might be annoyed and arguing but at least you're not ranting and getting yourself into a frenzy. So your aim is to stay on the lower steps; to stop and turn back when you find yourself heading for that top floor with all the trouble it can bring to you and to others. Keep this image in mind when you are getting annoyed and don't climb that stairs!

TIP When you're angry, visualise the anger stairs and stay on those lower steps – don't climb the stairs to the point where you do harm.

THIS CHAPTER'S TIPS

1. Always interrupt angry thoughts as soon as you spot them.
2. Instead of acting out your anger, simply describe what it is that you are angry about. In both the long and the short run, this approach is far more likely to get you the cooperation of other people.
3. Try to influence other people by all means, but drop the illusion that you can control their behaviour.
4. Prevent the escalation of anger by putting your attention on your physical experience.
5. When you're angry, visualise the anger stairs and stay on those lower steps – don't climb the stairs to the point where you do harm.

Notes
1. *Two false friends* in Chapter 1.
2. 'Confusing intentional and unintentional behaviour' in *Have a Good Day: Four Crucial Thinking Behaviours*, Chapter 4.

RELATIONSHIPS

Six tips for making them better

10

In this chapter
- Have fun
- Make quality time
- Learn to talk and to listen
- Start rows gently, end them with a gesture
- Ask for her help
- Be a mirror

Have fun

When Joe and Doris went to a marriage counsellor he asked them if they were having fun anymore. When they replied that they weren't he told them to arrange two dates with each other in the next week. Then he charged them. Joe and Doris had fun that week but they were a little miffed with the counsellor. After all, when you're paying out good money you expect something more complex than being told to have fun. They had to admit it was the first week in ages that they had had fun with each other, though, and that it had brought them closer.

Why is fun the first casualty of long-term relationships? The arrival of children disrupts a couple's social life and it takes work to put it back together again. Suddenly, getting to go out together becomes a challenge. It is all too easy to just let it go.

Even if there are no kids, it is easy to slip into familiar routines in which the fun slowly fades into the background. Conflict usually drives out fun. When a relationship gets a long way into the conflict zone, you will almost always find that the couple has stopped having fun. This is not always true. Some people manage to fight and have fun at the same time! But for many, the fun slowly but surely goes out of the conflicted relationship. What is left is a business relationship about kids and mortgages, punctuated by occasional fights.

One of the most important things you can do to put life back into your long-term relationship is to start having fun together again. There's more to fun than fun! Fun is a basic human need. In his Choice Theory, Dr William Glasser lists fun along with power, belonging, freedom and survival as the basic needs that drive our behaviour. Glasser argues that fun is related to learning. Small children learn through play. Play is fun. Glasser has noted, and you can check this out for yourself, that people who think they know everything are no fun!

Help your partner to have fun and you are helping them meet one of their basic needs. That's not a bad deal – have fun and meet a basic need at the same time! When you start having fun again you will notice something new. You will see aspects of your partner that you have long forgotten about. As a couple, you will be different when you are having fun to how you are in your daily life. You will regain at least some of the experience of each other that drew you together at the beginning of your relationship.

It is awfully easy, as a couple, to get locked into roles. How many parents end up calling each other Mammy and Daddy? It's only when you start to have fun again that the two people who fell in love and who wanted to be together forever step out of the shadows.

Be warned of two pitfalls though. The first is that having fun involves work. If you have children, babysitters have to be arranged; if you have no children you may have to navigate around each other's favourite TV programmes, meetings with friends, late working nights and other obstacles that life will gladly put in your path. Don't let the work put you off. See it as a small price to pay for the new life in your relationship.

The second pitfall is sabotage. If you are going through a tough time in your relationship, your demons will set about sabotaging your efforts to have fun. There you are, waiting for your partner to arrive so you can go to the movies and you get a call to say they're held up at work or stuck in traffic. Then the doorbell rings and it's your parents on an unexpected visit. Your partner then gets home to find you entertaining your in-laws for as long as they choose to stay. It's only a short step to a flaming row in which you each accuse the other of sabotaging the evening.

So you need to be aware that life likes to stick spanners in the works. When you set out to have fun you need to be extra tolerant of each other's faults when things go wrong. Chalk it up to the demons.

TIP The surest way to rediscover each other is to have fun again.

Make quality time

What we really need, said Joe and Doris to each other, is more quality time. So they decided to have quality time on Saturday afternoon at three o'clock. When Saturday afternoon arrived they looked at each other and both asked the same question: what the heck do we do now?

Nowadays quality time is thought of as a period of intense involvement sandwiched between the demands of work and home. This definition is an outcome of our efforts to cope with a world in which time is always in short supply. As a matter of fact, quality time probably ought to be kept short, as we'll see below. And it can be enormously helpful in deepening the relationship between partners.

But what does it mean and how do you do it? Doing quality time is a simple concept so long as you observe a few ground rules. It means that a couple is prepared to put their differences and routines aside for a short time in order to spend some satisfying time with each other. Making quality time has the great value that each person knows the other person has put this time aside to be with them. It is an affirmation of the value of one person by the other. If a relationship is in the conflict zone, quality time can remind both partners of what they are at risk of losing. If the relationship has gone stale, quality time, deliberately chosen, can bring new life to the interaction between the two.

Follow the guidelines below to create good quality time:

Do something you both like doing

Sounds obvious? You'd be surprised! Many a couple has fallen at the first hurdle with a row over whose favourite activity should benefit from quality time. The key is that quality time should be made up of doing something you both like doing. This could be as simple as going for a walk or to a movie; it could be cycling, cooking, driving, going to lunch in a restaurant or any one of hundreds of thousands of things.

Do something that requires effort

This guideline is written in this way to make the point that slumping in a semi-conscious state in front of a TV set does not constitute quality time. Why? Because if you are in conflict or if your relationship is stale you probably already spend much of your time together looking at the TV screen and not at each other. Of course, you might decide to watch a DVD for your quality time but beware – when you are watching television you are a sitting duck for kids, pets, pests, phone calls and casual visitors. So do yourselves a favour and exclude the TV from your quality time.

Don't mention the war

Remember that quality time is a very special period set aside to enhance your relationship. Frankly, if you start going over the things you fight about, that quality time is going to vanish in a flash, probably a flash of anger. So when you are having quality time, follow Basil Fawlty's advice: don't mention the war.

Don't criticise the other person during this period

If your quality time is taken up with criticising each other about your choice of clothes, how you drive, what you have picked from the menu etc. then it will quickly cease to be quality time. Quality time is special; it is not everyday life. So when you feel the need to criticise your partner, zip your lip. Safeguard the quality time. The world will survive without your criticisms during this period and you will both feel a lot better for it.

Choose an activity you can repeat

There's little point in having fifteen minutes of quality time once every ten years. If quality time is to work its magic on your relationship you'll need to do it quite often. Going to a hillside to watch the sun rise is probably not viable as a frequent activity – unless, of course, you live on a hill. Going for a walk in the park or having lunch together every Sunday afternoon is far more viable.

Keep it short

Fifteen minutes to a couple of hours is a realistic period for quality time. If you try to make quality time last for hours and hours, it will inevitably be sabotaged by the distractions, interruptions and conflicts of everyday living. You cannot put yourself in a bubble and isolate yourself from the world for any considerable length of time. Aim to keep periods of quality time relatively brief.

TIP Keep quality time short, cheap and simple and do it as often as you can.

Learn to talk and to listen

When Doris has a problem, Joe generates solutions. Doris, however, doesn't always implement his solutions and sometimes accuses Joe of not really listening to her. Joe resents this but has to admit he is impatient with everyday conversations which seem to go nowhere.

Men and women talk differently. We talk differently because talk has different meanings for us. These differences show themselves in our attitudes to two distinct types of conversation. The first type is the functional conversation, or conversation aimed at getting things done. The second is conversation as the expression of a relationship. There are many other types of conversation but these are the two that most often impinge on relationships.

We are all, men and women, familiar with functional conversation. What's the best route to the airport? Something is broken, how can I get it fixed? Where did you put the paint brushes? These questions and the conversations that might arise from them are functional. Their purpose is to get you to the airport, get something fixed or enable you to start painting.

Conversation as the expression of a relationship is different. In this conversation, two people talk simply as an expression of the fact that they have a relationship with each other. The only – but very important – function of the conversation is to acknowledge that relationship.

To an outsider, the conversation may sound quite trivial, but that is to mistake where the value of the conversation lies. The value of this kind of conversation does not lie in its content. Its value lies in the fact that two people, simply by having the conversation, are acknowledging that they are in a relationship with each other. Each person may listen to the other talking about how the day went but they are only listening because they have a relationship. If they didn't have a relationship they wouldn't be having this conversation. So what the conversation is about doesn't matter – what matters is that they are having the conversation at all.

The great divide between men and women tends to be that men undervalue that second kind of conversation – conversation as the expression of relationship. A man may see little point to talking about his day because, well, there is nothing that needs deciding and nothing that needs to be fixed. To the woman, however, talking about the day is part of the relationship she has with him. Men find this hard to understand.

This difference can be seen more clearly when the woman talks about, say, a problem at work. Long before she has finished explaining the problem, the man will have jumped in with his ideas for solving it. Oddly enough, this may leave the woman feeling she has not been listened to. Why? The woman wants the man to listen to her complaint but not in order to have him fix it. She wants a relationship conversation. She wants him to listen to her because he is her partner and they talk about things. The man, on the other hand, has gone straight into functional mode. He hears a problem and he suggests a solution. With the best will in the world, he has missed the point.

It is important to understand that this is not true of all men or of all women. It is also not true of any man or woman all the time. But it is true often enough to make a difference.

How can we men use this knowledge to enhance our relationships with women? By talking about things that do not need fixing or resolving. By talking about our opinions and our feelings about things even though we see no practical point to doing so. And by taking an interest when our partner is talking to us about her feelings and thoughts even if we see no great importance in the subject matter.

Let me emphasise that this has nothing to do with stupid old notions about women as chatterboxes. I think most men would agree that the deepest conversations they have ever had have been with women. It is simply a matter of the different ways in which the genders use conversation.

Failure to understand this difference leads to that sad scene in which two people sit together in the pub with nothing to say. It may be that the man will only talk about things that 'matter' and that the woman has learned that talking about anything else is a waste of time because she will not be listened to. We need to talk up and to realise that the talking may just be more important than what we are talking about. Indeed, as we will see later in this chapter, even the most seemingly trivial remarks can heal awkward situations.

When women talk about problems, whether emotional or practical, we need to learn to listen before we rush in with solutions. The fact is, in this world there very often is no solution and the solutions you suggest she may very well have thought of already. What she needs is for you to listen while she expresses how she feels. So we need to be ready to talk about stuff we would not ordinarily talk about and we need to listen when we would rather talk.

> **TIP** Remember, the fact that you are talking to her is of more importance to your partner than what you are talking about. And the fact that you are listening to her may be far more important than the tremendously important things you want to say.

Start rows gently, end them with a gesture

Harsh words and long silences used to be the essential features of rows between Joe and Doris. The silences were exhausting and it was only when the memory of the harsh words faded away that one or the other would move to end the silence. When they asked the counsellor how to stop fighting he told them they couldn't stop fighting: they were human beings and human beings were just too pig-headed to live in harmony all the time (he was a rather odd counsellor). What they needed to learn, he said, was to start and end their rows differently – then their relationship would improve.

In an emotional world, how we say a thing is at least as important as what we say. We can keep our relationships in good order by paying attention to the way we say things. In particular, when we want to express disagreement with our partner it is important to begin gently.

Some people always express disagreement harshly. Perhaps this is how it was done in their own home of origin. Or perhaps it is something they learned to do along their way through life. However, expressing disagreement harshly sours relationships. Harshness draws out an angry response from the other person. They will not always make that angry response in words but, hidden or not, it will be there.

Moreover harshness conveys an underlying message of contempt for the other person. That message, if repeated often enough, chips away at the foundations of the relationship.

If a couple at odds with each other wants to enhance their relationship, they would do well to agree that when they express disagreement they will begin gently. They would do well also to seek to end their rows as quickly as they can. Research done in the US by John and Julie Gottman into successful, long-term relationships suggest that couples whose relationships work are able to get over rows quickly.

Note that you are not being asked to avoid having rows. No matter how good your relationship is you are likely to fall out now and then. What matters, since most rows are about trivial issues anyway, is how quickly you can end the row and get back to being friends again. This doesn't mean you must resolve your rows quickly. Actually, the issues rows are about are usually neither resolved nor remembered. What matters is how quickly you can actually end the row and its aftermath.

Lengthy silences which go on for days or even weeks are exhausting, unpleasant and undermine the relationship. They come to be dreaded by both partners who, however, do not know how to bring them to an end. The longer the silence lasts, the harder it is to break. Finally, somebody begins to talk again and the ice is broken. But the cost has been high if the silence has gone on for a long time.

In successful relationships, the Gottmans' research suggests, one partner or other signals the end of hostilities with a simple gesture – not a physical gesture but a verbal one. A verbal gesture is a remark completely unrelated to the row. If you've had a fight over your attitude to her mother there may be nothing either of you can say on this issue to end the post-row ill feeling. But a conciliatory remark about something else can help – 'Do you want me to pick the kids up from school?' is an example. It can signal that hostilities are over and you want to be friends again.

Such a remark is a gesture. Other gestures could be:

- 'What would you like for dinner?'
- 'Do you want to go out tonight?'
- 'Do you want the newspaper?'
- 'Would you like a coffee?' etc.

The partner making the gesture signals that they want to be friends again without waiting for the argument to be resolved. The willingness to make gestures can decide whether the relationship survives and flourishes or whether it slowly falls apart.

TIP Express disagreement gently and use verbal gestures to end the tension that follows rows.

Ask for her help

Everybody sees Tony as a self-sufficient guy who knows all the answers. But Tony is hurting inside. His relationship with Margaret is growing more and more distant and he doesn't know what to do about it. Needless to say, Tony, being a self-sufficient guy, doesn't ask Margaret how to make their relationship better. In fact, he doesn't ask for help with anything, however trivial. That's a pity because asking for help could bring warmth back into his relationship with Margaret.

We men are notorious for our reluctance to ask for help. Some of us will drive for hours rather than stop and ask for directions. We can mull over a problem in our own minds for years without asking for the advice which could help solve it. I have met men whose relationships with their partners have withered and died over a few years but who have never spoken to them about what was going on in their hearts. And so a relationship ends which might have gone on to flourish had it been spoken about.

Perhaps we behave like this for the same reasons that we are more reluctant than women to go to a doctor when we feel unwell: we see ourselves as strong, not making a fuss and not displaying weakness. Needless to say this does not apply to all men. However, it applies to enough of us enough of the time to be important.

For that reason, men may be surprised to learn of one particular technique for enhancing relationships: ask for help. This can mean asking for help with simple things: what to do about a financial problem or a work problem, for instance, or even the best route from Point A to Point B! Or it may mean seeking your partner's help with a complex or serious problem: a health issue, perhaps.

Why should seeking help in this way serve to enhance relationships? Probably because it shows a respect for your partner's views. It also shows that you are not the big, strong man who knows everything and, believe it or not, your partner will respond to this in a positive way. Try it and see.

TIP Don't be the big strong man all the time: ask your partner for help – with anything – and it will bring you closer to each other.

Be a mirror
Conor always hopes Lynn will be in good humour when they get home from work. When she is cheerful, he feels great and enjoys his time with her. When she is angry or resentful, he finds himself becoming sulky and they often have rows. Actually, Lynn always hopes Conor will be in a good humour when they meet and for exactly the same reason. What neither realises is that they are mirroring each other's behaviour and that they can use this knowledge to make their relationship better.

In the Chapter 6 on depression, I described the discovery by scientists of mirror neurons. But a knowledge of mirror neurons can also transform your relationships. Actually, this concept is so important that it's worth refreshing our memory on what it means. What the scientists discovered was that our brains mirror each other's behaviour. When you are watching a football match, those parts of the brain that are used by the players to tell their feet to kick the ball, to run, to turn etc. are also activated in the spectators. Your brain mirrors what is going on in the brains of the players.

This may explain why teams have an advantage when playing at home: the encouragement and enthusiasm of the crowd is mirrored in the brains of the players.

Mirroring can occur with any physical behaviour you might observe. This ability may have evolved as an advantage for babies and children who do much of their learning by imitating other human beings.

What is most important for our purposes is that mirroring applies not only to physical activities but also to emotions. If you observe me being angry, those parts of your brain that are involved in feeling and expressing anger become active. If you observe me being loving then those parts of your brain that are involved in being loving become active.

Of course, there are exceptions. It is possible to resist or block the mirroring. The person described as 'distant' may be one who refuses to engage with other people's thoughts and feelings and who thereby avoids the influence of mirroring. But even there, mirroring can occur. We have all heard of the person – and perhaps we have been that person – who starts off an encounter by being distant or hostile but who eventually 'melts' under the influence of the other's warmth or charm. What has happened is that the other's warmth has activated those parts of the 'distant' person's brain that are associated with feeling warmth. This activated a feeling of friendliness on the part of that other person.

How can we use mirroring to enhance our relationships? We can begin by recognising that if I speak harshly or dismissively there is a strong possibility that I will create exactly those feelings in my partner. But if I speak with warmth and friendliness and if I persist in doing so even when my partner is annoyed with me, then there is a good chance that my partner will begin to experience the warmth and friendliness that I am conveying. Equally I can remember that if my partner is harsh or in a bad mood, then there will be a natural tendency on my part to fall into the same mindset of moodiness or harshness simply because my brain will tend to mirror what it sees my partner doing.

This understanding gives me a choice. Will I respond to anger with anger or will I respond with calm or warmth or love? The key point is that I have a choice about how I respond once I understand what is going on. By choosing to project warmth, I can enhance my relationship with my partner. Mirroring has always existed. Now that we know about it, why not use it to improve our relationships?

TIP Projecting warmth to your partner can have a powerful effect as her brain responds to the warmth she observes in you.

THIS CHAPTER'S TIPS

1. The surest way to rediscover each other is to have fun again.
2. Keep quality time short, cheap and simple and do it as often as you can.
3. Remember, the fact that you are talking to her is of more importance to your partner than what you are talking about. And the fact that you are listening to her may be far more important than the tremendously important things you want to say.
4. Express disagreement gently and use verbal gestures to end the tension that follows rows.
5. Don't be the big strong man all the time: ask your partner for help – with anything – and it will bring you closer to each other.
6. Projecting warmth to your partner can have a powerful effect as her brain responds to the warmth she observes in you.

MARRIAGE BREAKUP

Getting through

11

In this chapter
- Consider mediation
- Get your own legal advice
- Don't tell the kids you did it for them
- Kids and their friends
- Never complain to your kids about your ex
- Work at making new friends
- Beware of fighting to maintain a connection

The end of a marriage or long-term relationship brings with it a mixture of feelings of anger, shame, loss, resentment and regret. Sometimes these feelings persist for longer than either ex-partner expects. Writers on this issue speak of an 'off the wall year' after a marriage ends. During this year or so, you veer between normality, rage, elation and depression, entirely unsure as to which it will be from day to day.

The 'off the wall year' may last for less than a year or more than a year but it will eventually end. The fact that it will end is hard to believe when you are in the middle of the pain of a marriage breakup but it is a belief that you need to cling onto in your darkest moments. As you see-saw between emotions, remind yourself that one day this vortex of feelings will end and you will be able to see clearly again.

What follows are some guidelines to help you deal with the experience of breakup and its consequences in a way that does not make matters worse than they have to be.

Consider mediation
When John and Rachel broke up, each went to good, tough lawyers to help them fight their corner. Solicitors' letters flew back and forth. As they did

so, the anger and bitterness between John and Rachel grew. In the end, issues of finance, access and custody were settled on the steps of the court. John pays Rachel support for their children and sees them every weekend. However, the bitterness between himself and Rachel has never gone away. They have not spoken a word to each other for three years.

Mediation is a process aimed at helping people whose marriages are breaking up to reach agreement on the arrangements concerning money and children. The aim is to avoid adding the extra bitterness and expense that fighting it out through lawyers can involve.[1] In this process, the couple meets with a mediator three to six times for about an hour at a time. They look at the financial needs, income and outgoings for both of them now and in the future, at what might work in terms of support payments, and at issues concerning property and pensions. If they have children, they look at access to the children, how to reach decisions on the children's education, how to handle holiday periods and so on. The aim is for both parties to reach an agreement which they believe is as fair and as workable as is possible in the circumstances.

Usually, when they arrive at a draft agreement each will bring it to their own solicitor who may recommend changes which, again, can be agreed in the mediation process. If the couple wish, the final agreement can become a legally binding document. Experience has shown that mediated agreements are more likely to be observed than arrangements made in court. The big benefit, however, is the avoidance of the bitterness and expense that can be involved in a legal battle.

That doesn't mean mediation is easy. The likelihood is that there will be anger and bitterness in the room. Issues such as money and children are highly emotional. The two people separating are already in a swirl of painful emotions – so do not expect a calm discussion. Nevertheless, mediation can help you avoid years of conflict. It provides a forum in which you can both look at difficult issues. Painful as it may be, for instance, the question of how to work out where the children will spend Christmas Day is better addressed in the mediation room than on your ex-wife's doorstep.

> **TIP** If you're separating, put to your partner the possibility of a mediated agreement. If they refuse there is little you can do about that. But if they agree, you will both be better off for it.

Get your own legal advice

Max is really worried. He is separating from Ellen and she says her lawyer says she will be able to take his business away from him and that unless he agrees to her financial demands he will never see the children again. On the other hand, one of Max's workmates, who has been through all this himself, has told Max that the way to handle the negotiations about money is to cut off all financial support for Ellen and the children. Max doesn't like this either. It is not in his nature to be vicious. But what else is he to do?

When a marriage breaks up, legal rights and responsibilities suddenly take on a huge emotional charge. People who have never before had to think about issues of custody, access and financial support now think of little else for days, weeks or months. These are tough and painful issues. However, they will be much easier to handle if both parties will take two pieces of advice to heart:

1. Don't take your legal advice from your partner's lawyer
2. Don't take your legal advice from your friends or drinking buddies.

It is quite common for one or the other party in a marriage breakup to claim that their lawyer is saying this, that or the other about financial and other rights. Usually what the lawyer is alleged to have said is to the advantage of the speaker and to the disadvantage of the dismayed listener. It is very important to understand that what you are hearing is a highly biased and coloured account of what your partner's lawyer said. All sorts of extraordinary nonsense is attributed to lawyers by partners trying to get an advantage over other partners or by partners who misunderstand what is being said to them. Unless your partner's lawyer is actually in the room saying it, don't believe it.

Please do yourself the favour of getting your own legal advice. That legal advice may be surprisingly different to the story that was told you by your partner. If you can't afford to go to a lawyer, consider going to a service such as that provided by a non-governmental organisation.[2]

The other great source of misinformation is the colleague or drinking partner. These people can tell you in great detail, and with great conviction, what to do – and what they tell you to do will very often make matters worse. You must remember that they are not the ones who have to live with the consequences of what you do. To them, it's all a bit like going to a boxing match and encouraging the contestants to give each other a good hiding.

Accept their sympathy by all means – we all need a shoulder to cry on at a time like this – but for heaven's sake, don't take legal advice from them. You may as well take poison!

TIP Take your legal advice only from your own lawyer or from an organisation set up to provide such advice. Never take your legal advice from your partner, your pals or your workmates.

Don't tell the kids you did it for them

When Tom and Rose broke up after two years of fighting, they faced the dilemma of how to explain this to their children. Now that they were breaking up, they themselves were able to deal with each other reasonably civilly. They agreed that the best approach to take with the children was to say that they were doing it for their sake, that it was unfair on the children to have to put up with their rows and that they believed this would provide the children with a better life into the future. The children were distraught. Their daughter became angry and rebellious and her relationship with her parents broke down eventually. Their son cried and then became silent and depressed. He told his friends that it was his fault his parents' marriage had broken up.

It is vital to avoid a situation in which your children blame themselves for the breakup of your marriage. That they might do so seems strange to the adult mind but the teenager who was in conflict with the parents or the child who is reprimanded – perhaps reasonably – for bad behaviour before the announcement of the breakup can very easily make that link.

Therefore, in telling the children why you are separating, it is terribly important for the parents to take the responsibility onto their own shoulders and not to inadvertently pass it on to the children. Avoid the classic mistake of telling the children that you are doing this for their sake. After all, to say that you're doing it for their sake implies that if they were not there you would not be breaking up. That is a heavy burden to place on their shoulders.

Do, however, assure them that you will always be their parents and that you will always work together to make sure that they are okay.

TIP Never tell the children that you are splitting up for their sake. To do so is to put a responsibility on their shoulders that belongs on yours.

Kids and their friends

Michael's son and daughter stay with him every weekend from Saturday morning to Sunday evening. Lately, it has happened a few times that the children, who are close in age, have skipped the visit. According to his ex-wife, this was because friends had invited them to concerts, birthday parties and other social events. Michael has no doubt that his ex-wife is putting them up to this and the pain of it has increased the bitterness between them. Some of that anger is carried over to Michael's interactions with the children when they come to stay with him. The result is sulking on the part of both Michael and the children and an unpleasant time for all.

When parents separate, their children's time is rationed between them. Most of that time will be spent with the parent with whom they are living – usually the mother. The demands of school and home life put a boundary on the amount of time the children can spend with the parent who is living away from the family home. This time, then, is precious because there is relatively little of it – so when a visit is cancelled, fathers can hardly be blamed for feeling angry and suspicious.

It is vital to remember, however, that as children get older, the prospect of spending weekends with either parent will become less attractive. A party organised by a pal will be correspondingly more attractive. It isn't that they have stopped loving either parent; it is just that the children are at that stage of their lives developmentally when they are seeking to separate from the parents and become individual persons in their own right. This doesn't mean they want to ditch the parents! They are caught in a dilemma – they want to be with them and away from them at the same time.

All this can be hurtful for the parent who has left the family home. However, the needs of the children must be taken into account and a little creative thinking can help that parent to meet his needs as well. Perhaps he can give the children a lift to and from the event or perhaps he can meet them for something to eat during the week. You can come up with solutions like this once you realise that the children's wish to spend time with their friends is not necessarily part of a conspiracy by their mother.

All this will work better, by the way, if there is a reasonably cooperative relationship between the separated parents. Then, conspiracy theories are less likely to arise and creative solutions are more likely to emerge.

> **TIP** Accept that as the children grow up, they may not want to come to you every weekend but that you can still be involved with their lives.

Never complain to your kids about your ex

Both Tim and Sheila have found that, even as adults, their children are still angry at them over their breakup. In particular, they become angry if either one of them mentions the other. Eventually each finds out that the children have never forgotten how their parents complained to them about each other's failings. They hated hearing this because they wanted to be loyal to both parents. Yet they had to listen to the latest twists and turns in the everlasting conflict between their parents, until they were old enough to be able to refuse to listen anymore.

If there is one thing that children of separated parents detest, it is listening to each parent criticising the other. It is of the utmost importance to avoid this practice so as to reduce the emotional impact on the children and to preserve your future relationship with them. Neither do children want to be the go-betweens who convey demands and complaints from one parent to the other.

Adopt the rule that if you have something to say to the other parent, you will say it directly to them yourself or you will not say it at all. This rule applies especially if what you have to say to the other parent is critical of that parent. The children are a product of both parents and feel loyalty to both. To criticise the other parent to the children is to criticise the source of half your children's genetic makeup. It is not all that far removed from criticising the children themselves.

Open conflict between separated parents is hurtful and sometimes frightening to the children. Usually, there is no need for the children to know about these rows and spats and you will be a better parent if you spare them that knowledge.

> **TIP** Never complain to your children about the other parent and never ask them to carry criticisms and demands back and forth.

Work at making new friends

When Andrew and Janet split up, Andrew assumed he would create a new circle of friends for himself with reasonable ease. But it was harder than he thought. Most of their friends had either been Janet's friends originally or they had been parents of children who were going to school or other activities with their children. Without children, and the need for families to cooperate with getting kids to and from school and extracurricular activities, Andrew found it difficult to make friends.

Some people still live in communities, mainly rural, in which there are permanent networks of friends, relatives and acquaintances. Whatever happens in their marriage, they will always have someone to talk to and socialise with. Most of us are not so fortunate. We live in an individualised society in which we barely know the people next door. In such a society, it is very often the needs of children that bring people together.

Children must be got to school, brought home from school, minded and fed and driven to and from music, swimming, dancing, speech and drama, football and all the rest of it. Needless to say, this requires a lot of cooperation between various parents who could be forgiven for feeling that it would be easier to run a multi-national corporation! More often than not, it is through this cooperation that couples actually make friends in the neighbourhood.

Therefore, if you're separating from your spouse and if the children will not be living with you most of the time, you will not be able to rely on this source of new friends. You will need to work at your social life by renewing connections with old friends, getting involved in sports, cultural and political events. You will need to work at it – it won't happen by itself.

> **TIP** Separated parents must work at making new friends, especially if they no longer have small children to make friends for them.

Beware of fighting to maintain a connection

Four years after their split, Matthew and Jane are still at each other's throats about issues big and small – where the children should be educated, Matthew's tone of voice on the phone the other night, how Jane 'slammed' the door when Matthew was collecting the kids and so on. Each talks endlessly to their friends about the other's crimes and misdemeanours. Their friends wish they would just get over each other.

Counsellors and friends of separated people will often have come across the can't-stop-hating-you syndrome in which the ex-partners seem to occupy more of each other's lives after they split up than before. Every little act of selfishness by one partner is magnified by the other into an act of monstrous greed. Arrangements concerning children inevitably seem to go wrong. Agreements about maintenance or the upkeep of the family home generate row after row.

The result is almost daily rows between the ex-partners. Friends on each side are treated to the minute details of these quarrels. Some so-called friends make matters worse by urging retaliation; others, those with lives of their own, long for a break in the saga.

Sometimes what's going on is that one partner is mistreating the other. In that case, the partner who is being mistreated may need to see a solicitor. What can also be happening, though, is that the couple is maintaining a connection with each other by fighting. After all, the rows mean they still have contact several times a week or even every day. Without the rows there might be no contact. The rows bring an intense emotional connection which, though painful, may hurt less than no connection at all.

If you think this might be happening in your separation, consider whether it is possible to have a different relationship with your partner or ex-partner. Consider whether you would not be better off getting on with your life while they get on with theirs.

You will find many techniques elsewhere in this book to help you to deal more effectively with the emotions aroused by quarrels with your ex-partner. Is not an easy process and you may need to go to a counsellor for help, but it could be worthwhile and it could open up a whole new future for you.

> **TIP** If you're still fighting with your ex-partner after all these years, consider whether you might be doing so because you have failed to move out emotionally.

THIS CHAPTER'S TIPS

1. If you're separating, put to your partner the possibility of a mediated agreement. If she refuses there is little you can do about that. But if she agrees, you will both be better off for it.
2. Take your legal advice only from your own lawyer or from an organisation set up to provide such advice. Never take your legal advice from your partner, your pals or your workmates.
3. Never tell the children that you are splitting up for their sake. To do so is to put a responsibility on their shoulders that belongs on yours.
4. Accept that as the children grow up, they may not want to come to you every weekend but that you can still be involved with their lives.
5. Never complain to your children about the other parent and never ask them to carry criticisms and demands back and forth.
6. Separated parents must work at making new friends, especially if they no longer have small children to make friends for them.
7. If you're still fighting with your ex-partner after all these years, consider whether you might be doing so because you have failed to move out emotionally.

Notes

1. In Ireland, a Free Family Mediation Service is run by the Family Support Agency (www.fsa.ie). Aim Family Services (www.aimfamilyservices.ie), an experienced non-governmental organisation, also has a mediation service. In the UK, ask your Citizen's Advice Bureau for information on the mediation service.
2. Aim Family Services' website at www.aimfamilyservices.ie contains excellent information on issues surrounding marriage breakup. Every person who is facing into this situation should read the information there. In the UK, your Citizen's Advice Bureau can help with this information.

CRITICS AND OTHER PESTS

Dealing with difficult people

12

In this chapter
- One principle, three choices
- Techniques for dealing with criticism
- Try saying 'No'!

One principle, three choices
Jerry works in the family business with his older brother, who has always assumed the role of boss. His brother is dismissive of Jerry, who is miserable but sees no way out.

Frank and Margaret live with his parents. His parents' drinking leads to rows between them and their son and daughter-in-law. When Frank and Margaret try to talk to his parents about this when they are sober, they refuse to discuss it. The young couple have reached the stage at which they need to make a choice about what to do.

Difficult people abound in life. Who knows: you may be one yourself! Indeed, it may be more accurate to talk about difficult behaviours than difficult people. The person who is difficult to you may be a delight to someone else.

What is a difficult behaviour? For the purposes of this chapter, a person who is aggressive and intrusive, perhaps consistently rude is engaging in a difficult behaviour. Or your difficulty may be with someone who stonewalls you when you try to talk to them, who is negative all the time, who seems to suck the energy out of the room and everybody in it. Others may be totally inconsistent and disorganised about what they want when things need to be done and so on – this can be disruptive in the workplace as well as in relationships. It is especially disruptive if you are the poor sod who is expected to make up for someone else's disorganised behaviour!

When dealing with difficult people, there is one principle to keep in mind and three choices – and only three – that we can make.

One principle

Here is a key principle: Changing other people's behaviour is not in my power to do. I can try to influence other people and sometimes this will work. However, controlling another person's behaviour for more than a short period of time is not in my power. I am the only person whose behaviour I can control.

Human beings have a peculiar characteristic. We can spend years in unhealthy relationships in the home, the workplace or socially in the belief that we can change the behaviour of other people. Yet every day, life teaches us that we cannot control the behaviour of others. Even the most terrifying dictators must fight an endless battle against those who will not agree to be controlled by them.

Though our experience tells us the belief is false and though it traps us in unhappiness, it can take years for the penny to drop. When the penny drops – and you may as well let it drop now! – you can make a clear choice. That choice will be one of the three outlined below.

The three choices

The three choices are: do nothing; stay in the situation but try to improve it; leave. Any of the three can be valid in certain situations at certain times.

Do nothing

Why might you stay in a relationship or workplace in which you are subjected to other people's unpleasant behaviours and be right? Here are some possibilities:

- some men stay with abusive partners because they want to protect their children

- you might put up with a bullying boss because you need the money to support yourself and your family
- you may be caring for a family member who is consistently rude and dismissive but who will not be around for very much longer.

Therefore, there are reasons for staying around people with difficult behaviours. But unless you are actually a saint, the emotional and health cost can be high. So if you are doing this, be clear that you are making a choice and that it won't go on forever. Knowing that staying and doing nothing is a choice will make it easier to bear. One day the children will have grown up, a better job will emerge elsewhere or the person you are caring for may go into long-term residential care or perhaps die.

In the example at the start of this section, Jerry is doing nothing about his older brother's behaviour towards him, but this isn't working for him. If Jerry continues doing what he's doing – which is nothing – he will keep on getting what he's got. Jerry needs to do something. But what? Well, he can make a start by choosing from among the options outlined below.

Stay in the situation but try to improve it
Most of us will try to improve a situation before we give up on it. Sometimes our attempts will work and sometimes they won't. One or more of the following options may help to bring about change for the better:

- Improve your own attitudes and/or behaviour. Very often this is the only thing you can do and it is very effective. For instance, you may need to increase your own tolerance for other people's behaviour. If the other person is making legitimate requests, however rudely, you may need to change your own attitude. If you are caring for a person who makes life difficult for you, it may be necessary for your own well-being to make arrangements to take regular time off – that's a change in behaviour. However, be careful that you don't use this option to keep you in an abusive, no-win situation that you really ought to leave.

- Seek improvements in the other person's behaviour. Remember the key principle that you cannot control another person's behaviour. You can, however, *ask* the other person to change. We have less insight into our behaviour than we think, and if you point out to someone that their behaviour upsets you, it may come as a surprise to them. If so, there is a good chance they will change their behaviour. If Jerry talks to his brother about how he feels, he may find that his brother will change his ways. If not, Jerry can take steps to increase his options (see next paragraph) and perhaps prepare to leave. By the way, when asking another person to change, you can improve your chances of a happy outcome by making your request politely and gently – harshness begets harshness.
- Increase your options. What other jobs are available? What can you do to get by if you leave an abusive social or family situation? Who can help you deal with the problem? Just knowing that you have options can sweep away the feeling of being trapped and make you more confident and effective. This is so, even if you never take up the options. This is the step Frank and Margaret now need to take. They have tried asking for change but it hasn't worked. Knowing they have options will empower them. It will give them a sense of assurance they lack right now and it may offer them a way out of the trap in which they find themselves.
- Seek help, from friends, a trade union, a manager, a solicitor, a counsellor etc. Many of us are afraid to ask for help and try to go it alone. This fear can keep us trapped. Even if you see no way out, remember that another person with another perspective can see choices you cannot see.

Leave

Yes, leave. Why are people so reluctant to take this option when it becomes the only viable one available? A key inhibition to leaving, I suspect, is the fear of what will happen next. The abusive situation is predictable and may even provide a strange sort of security. You may fear in the back of your mind that if you leave, whatever control you now have over your life will disappear. Ultimately, you have to ask yourself which matters more: your fear of what will happen if you leave or your knowledge of what will happen if you stay?

It also makes sense to adopt the motto: never leave until you have prepared your exit. The purpose of preparing is to give you as much control as you can get after you leave. For instance, don't leave a job until you have got another; before you leave home find another place to live; before you leave a relationship get back in touch with your friends. Sometimes this also means checking out your legal rights before you leave. And please do check out your legal rights with a lawyer or with an agency that specialises in helping people with your particular issue. The chap sitting across the desk from you or beside you in the bar is simply not a reliable source of legal information!

TIP Look at the three choices you have in a difficult situation: do nothing; stay and ask for change; leave. Consider carefully which of these choices will best work for you and for those you care about.

Techniques for dealing with criticism

Malcolm's wife Elizabeth had a stroke shortly after he retired. Now caring for Elizabeth is his full-time occupation. Elizabeth's sister who lives nearby visits twice a week and criticises Malcolm's caring relentlessly. Malcolm listens with a mixture of shame and anger and tries to defend himself. But Elizabeth's sister is skilled at debate and Malcolm ends up feeling full of guilt. He desperately wants to be able to defeat Elizabeth's sister in an argument and to convince her that he is a good carer. Meanwhile, her visits upset him so much he sometimes throws up before she arrives.

Nobody likes criticism – not even 'constructive' criticism. Some criticism is worth listening to. It may be justified. Even if mistaken, it may be well meant. What this section is concerned with, however, is the critic who criticises out of their own inner anger or out of pleasure in putting people down. It is helpful, for your own peace of mind, to choose an attitude towards such critics so that they no longer upset you. The techniques below will help you to do that.

Take the sails out of their wind

Sailing boats take down their sails in a storm. So rather than fight the wind, and get turned over, they let the wind blow by. This is an excellent metaphor for an assertive way to deal with the kind of criticism that gives you no useful information but simply allows the critic to beat you up. When you try to respond directly to such criticism you can be like a boat in a storm – you get tossed around and you make no headway.

Instead you can choose a response. The response you choose depends on the situation. One response is to sidestep the criticism with an acknowledgement that the critic is right and you are wrong; a second is to acknowledge that some part of what the critic says might be right and leave it at that; a third is to ask the critic to expand on their criticisms. I call these approaches acknowledging, clouding and probing.

Doesn't sound very robust does it? However, a direct, robust response often provides the critic with still more energy and ammunition. Acknowledging, clouding and probing, on the other hand, aim to take the wind out of the critic's sails.

Here are some examples:

Acknowledge

If they're right just say so. Critic: *'Here you go again. You're late with that order. It should have been ready yesterday.'* You: *'You're right, I'm late.'* No need for a big argument about this. Acknowledge it and let it go.

Cloud

Agree with a bit of what they're saying: Critic: *'What's up with you? You're working all the time, you have no time for your friends, you're at it day and night, I don't know what's become of you.'* You: *'Yes, I'm working a lot'* or *'You may be right'.* That reply can be used for all sorts of criticism: Critic: *'It'll never work: they'll never agree to let you do this tomorrow instead of today.'* By replying, *'You may be right',* you leave the critic with their opinion and save yourself the bother of having to defend yourself.

Probe

Pick out one part of the criticism and ask a question starting with, *'What is it that bothers you about …?'* In this way you seek clarification and make it clear that the bad feeling belongs to the critic and not to you. Critic: *'You never take part in our staff meetings. What's the point in being there?'* You: *'What exactly is it that bothers you about me being quiet?'*

No monkeys need apply

Think of the critic's anger, sarcasm or bitterness as a monkey which is on the critic's back and which they are trying to pass on to you. Decide that you are not in the market for monkeys today. If you let the critic pass anger, sadness or guilt on to you then you have taken the monkey off the critic's back and put it on your own. So remind yourself to leave the monkey where he belongs: on the critic's shoulder!

Ask for what you want

To avoid criticising others unfairly and damagingly, cultivate the art of asking for what you want. Instead of asking, *'Why is it that every single time I want the sugar I have to ask for it? Isn't it about time you realised that I take sugar in my tea and that after you've helped yourself you should pass it on to me? But no, you're so wrapped up in your own little world you never think about anybody else. I might as well be dead for all you care'* try simply saying, *'Pass the sugar please'.*

> **TIP** You don't have to respond to unfair criticism with shame or anger. Instead, use the techniques above to manage how you respond to critics.

Try saying 'No'!

Kevin's son has never really taken to the idea of working. Kevin supports him and pays for his PlayStation games, his clothes, his broadband and other necessities. To do this, Kevin has to deny himself the pleasures in life that he would like. He even does extra work on Saturday mornings to help pay for the lifestyle of his son who is usually asleep at that time. Kevin's friends have told him to say 'No' to his son's requests for money but Kevin cannot bring himself to do this.

If the whole concept of saying 'No' is one that scares you then you can be particularly open to exploitation by difficult people. Actually, most of us seem to find it difficult to say 'No'. Not only do we find it difficult to say 'No' but we then give ourselves a hard time because of our reluctance to say 'No'! We accuse ourselves of being wimps and fools and all sorts of other unpleasant things. Talk about a no-win situation!

A reluctance to say 'No' is entirely understandable. We are social creatures. We need each other's cooperation. If we all went around saying 'No' all the time we would get little or no cooperation from each other. So our reluctance to say 'No' has its uses. Nevertheless, there are times when we all walk ourselves into trouble and hassle by saying 'Yes' when we know perfectly well that we ought to say 'No'. Below are a few tips which will help you to say 'No' when you need to.

Give them a hearing

In industrial relations settings, good negotiators never just say 'No'. They listen to what the other side has to say, to how the other side feels and, if necessary, they will spend a morning or a day or, in some circumstances, months listening to the other side's point of view and explaining their own. They know that what people want most of all, at a human level, is a hearing. Give people a good hearing and you will be surprised how often your 'No' is accepted – with gratitude for the hearing!

Practice 'Yes when', 'Yes if' and 'Yes but'

This is a particularly useful tactic, especially in the workplace, though it can also help in other situations. Suppose the people who allocate work to you do so in a disorganised fashion, leaving you with more to do at the end of the day than you can get around to doing in your working hours. Suppose also that you find it difficult to say 'No' to them and that indeed they would not welcome the idea of you saying 'No'. In this case you could try the 'Yes when', 'Yes if' and 'Yes but' approach:

- **Yes** I will look after this report for you **when** I have finished the report for the managing director.
- **Yes** I can get this item delivered now **if** the item you gave me earlier today can wait until tomorrow.
- **Yes** I can go to the meeting with the Finance Department **but** that means I will not be able to get this piece of work done today.

In this way you gain some degree of control without ever having to use the *no* word. This tactic could make a big difference to Kevin, too. 'Yes, I'll pay for the broadband when you've begun that Preparation for Work course you've been offered,' for instance.

Practice saying, 'I would prefer'

Instead of saying 'No' straight out, state a preference. In reply to, 'Can I come and stay with you for three months when I'm in Ireland?' you could say, 'You can certainly come for a week but I would prefer to help you to find another place after that'. Thinking in terms of preferences can help you to come up with choices that can meet some of your needs and some of the other person's needs. It gives you options that might not otherwise occur to you.

Remind yourself that people need more than they ask for

A person who asks you for, say, a loan doesn't just want the money. Like everybody they want to be treated with respect, given a hearing, accepted for what they are. So if you are not going to give them one of these four things – the money – you can give them the other three by giving them a hearing and by the way in which you state your refusal or preference. You'd be surprised at the difference it can make.

What's wrong with white lies?

Nothing! I realise that this statement would get me thrown out of assertiveness class but white lies really do have their place SOMETIMES if you want to say 'No' without hurting the other person. What's wrong with saying you have to work late tonight as a diplomatic way of getting out of a proposed date? What's wrong with saying you have a lodger in your spare room and won't therefore be able to give free board and lodgings for six months to your third cousin ten times removed who's coming over from New Zealand? Nothing at all! Be careful, however, and remember the proverb: a lie cannot stand on its own legs.

TIP Remember there's more than one way to say 'No'.

THIS CHAPTER'S TIPS

1. Look at the three choices you have in a difficult situation: do nothing; stay and ask for change; leave. Consider carefully which of these choices will best work for you and for those you care about.
2. You don't have to respond to unfair criticism with shame or anger. Instead, use the techniques above to manage how you respond to critics.
3. Remember there's more than one way to say 'No'.

WORKPLACE BULLYING

Taking care of yourself

13

In this chapter
- Limit the damage done by the workplace bully
- Basic steps if you are being bullied
- Taking responsibility
- Safeguarding mind and body
- The crusader trap

Limit the damage done by the workplace bully

We seem to be experiencing an epidemic of workplace bullying. Complaints flood in to trade unions and human resources departments; bullying cases appear with increasing frequency in the courts and before tribunals; and doctors and counsellors have become all too familiar with clients' stories of being bullied. But what is it? This is the definition currently used in Irish industrial relations:

> Workplace Bullying is repeated inappropriate behaviour, direct or indirect, whether verbal, physical or otherwise, conducted by one or more persons against another or others, at the place of work and/or in the course of employment, which could reasonably be regarded as undermining the individual's right to dignity at work.[1]

Insults, sneering, pushing, sabotage, impossible workloads and public humiliation all form part of bullying behaviour. Because we human beings are rather rough and ready and have all sorts of sharp edges, it is possible for us to engage in all the above behaviours at least once. Generally speaking, though, a single incident of this kind may not be bullying in the most damaging sense of that word. Damaging, inappropriate behaviour becomes bullying when it is repeated. It is the repetition of the behaviour that threatens to demoralise its target. By the way, I much prefer the word 'target' to 'victim': to think of yourself as a victim is to hand the bully their first victory.

This chapter does not deal with grievance procedures or with the law as it relates to bullying. Its whole focus is to enable you to maintain your emotional and physical well-being should you ever become a target of bullying. Let me put this more starkly; my message to you is:

Never cooperate with a bully by destroying your own mental and/or physical health.

An odd message? I don't believe so. I have met too many people who have been devastated by workplace bullying. Some are so devastated by it that even succeeding in a complaint against the bully doesn't seem to help them regain their equilibrium. I believe that much of that devastation arises from the endless replaying of scenes of bullying in the target's head and from attitudes that make matters worse. I will explain more of this later.

Basic steps if you are being bullied

First let's look at some basic steps to take if you are being bullied:

- Ask your colleagues if they, too, are being bullied. If you find that other people are being bullied you can support each other in taking joint action.
- Remember that research shows workplace bullies usually pick on people who are good at their job and who have high standards – remind yourself of this to reduce the emotional toll on your confidence.
- Write down an account of the bullying behaviour including:
  - What was said or done to you
  - When and where it happened
  - How you felt

- – Whether there were witnesses
- – How the bullying is affecting your health and well-being.

This account will be of importance if and when you make a complaint.

- Ask the bully to stop. This can be very effective if the other person does not realise they are bullying you. Asking the bully to stop is one of the earliest steps you should take to deal with this behaviour. A few pointers:
  - – Don't use the word 'bullying' or you will end up in an argument about the meaning of the word. Instead describe the behaviour of the bully, for example, 'I want you to stop shouting at me in public. If you are not happy with my work I want you to tell me in private'.

However, if the bullying continues you will need to say at a future meeting or by letter that you feel you are being bullied – otherwise they will be able to claim that there was no indication anything was wrong.

  - – Be calm, polite and firm – otherwise the bully may make a complaint of bullying against you.
  - – Make sure to see the bully in private and not where their supporters are around.
  - – Immediately after the meeting make a note of what happened and what was said. Write down the date and the time.
  - – If you feel unable to confront the bully in person, write a letter or memo. Make sure to stay calm and polite in your language so that you cannot later be accused of harassment.
- Talk to a union officer who can advise and support you.
- Talk to someone in authority whom you trust. This could be a manager or the human resources department.
- Share your feelings with family and friends. You need their support at this time. Don't fall into the trap of talking about nothing else but the bullying, however. This is not good for you or them.
- Beware of drinking too much and/or eating too little as you go through this distressing time. You need your health to get you through.

- See your GP. A week or two off work may give you time to gather your strength and reflect on what to do. Beware, however, of taking too much time off – sitting at home brooding about what is going on will not help you.
- If your employer has a confidential counselling scheme, make use of it. Otherwise, consider going to a private counsellor. The Irish Association for Counselling and Psychotherapy (Tel. 01-2300061) can give you the name of an accredited counsellor in your area.
- If you feel that staying in the job will seriously damage your health, talk to a union officer before you make a decision to leave and use the grievance procedure if there is one. I am assuming here that you have talked to the bully as described above and that your attempts to resolve the issue in this informal way have not worked. Informal solutions are almost always better than formal investigations and procedures, which can be lengthy and exhausting.

Taking responsibility

When Robert went to a counsellor he complained that a bully at work had destroyed his mental health. 'No,' the counsellor replied, 'safeguarding your mental health is your job, not the bully's.' Robert didn't like to hear this but it was true.

Remember I said earlier that the following advice was at the heart of this section of the book?

Never cooperate with a bully by destroying your own mental and/or physical health.

Bullying can destroy the confidence of targets for months and sometimes years. People bullied out of the workforce can find it hard to return because of the fear that it will happen again. In an Irish survey by the Anti-Bullying Centre at Trinity College Dublin, 25 per cent of targets said they had been seriously affected by being bullied.

This is why I am urging you to put taking care of your own mental and physical health at the top of your agenda.

People who are bullied tend to be good at their jobs and to have high standards of behaviour. Therefore they tend to be bewildered that they are bullied. It plays on their mind – *and that mental anguish can have detrimental effects if left unchecked.*

Envy and resentment are strong motivators for bullies. Bullies have a need to dominate, either directly or in 'sneaky' ways, which may reflect their own insecurities. Bullies may see themselves as 'robust' managers. Most bullying is done by immediate superiors. However, colleagues can bully too, as can subordinates. An aggressive management style facilitates bullying. Superiors and colleagues of a person who is newly employed may bully the newcomer. Men and women are equally capable of being bullies.

All these forms of bullying are deeply upsetting. My guess is that bullying by colleagues – to whom you would normally look for support – is worst of all. Again, in the face of this mental and physical upset, it is vital that you look after your own mental and physical health.

At worst, bullying can lead to the following symptoms in the target:

- **Physiological**: Sleeplessness, loss of energy, loss of appetite, high blood pressure, upset stomach
- **Psychological**: Anger, anxiety, panic attacks, depression, feeling isolated, suicidal thoughts
- **Behavioural**: Aggression, irritability, drinking or taking drugs, hypersensitivity to criticism, talking endlessly about the bullying etc.

Indeed, it can and does happen that even an investigation which finds in favour of the target of bullying leaves that person still feeling devastated. That is why it is so vital that you safeguard your own health when you are being bullied.

> **TIP** Never give responsibility for your physical and mental health to a bully.

Safeguarding mind and body

William used to be a good-humoured and interesting man until he was bullied at work. Now his memories of the bullying torment him. He cannot sleep at night and is always exhausted. He is no longer interesting: he talks only about the bullying. His good humour disappeared ages ago. He is suffering physically from too much drink, too little food and sleep deprivation.

Guard your mind

Two and a half thousand years ago, the Buddha warned that those who fill their own thoughts with the wrongs that have been done to them cannot be happy. To be happy you must stop filling your head with the wrongs done by others, he advised. Note that he is not asking you to pretend they never existed. Neither is he asking you to pretend that they don't matter. He is asking you to avoid replaying your grievances in your mind for the sake of your own mental health and happiness.

In the twentieth century, South African anti-apartheid campaigner Steve Biko said:

> The most potent weapon in the hands of the oppressor is the mind of the oppressed.

This is a remarkable statement and one worth remembering. Biko also was not a man who denied that injustices were done. Nor was he a man who sat back and did nothing about injustice: he died in police custody for his activities opposing the apartheid regime. However, like the Buddha, he understood the importance of guarding your own mind.

How is this to be done? When you spot yourself replaying the scenes of bullying, return to the present moment – to what you're hearing, seeing, doing. When you spot yourself imagining future scenes of bullying or revenge, return to the present moment.

If you are physically angry – face flushed, a feeling of 'fire in your belly' for instance – just notice the physical feeling without getting caught up in thoughts about it. Similarly if you are feeling tense or fearful, just notice the physical feeling without getting caught up in the thoughts. Notice how the physical feeling rises to a peak and then falls away. All the time, keep bringing yourself back into the moment whenever you begin to get caught by your thoughts.

The worldwide self-help movement, Recovery Inc, describes the process of getting caught in thoughts of anger or pain as 'imagination on fire'. It's a good phrase to remember. When your imagination is on fire you cannot have peace of mind. So when you notice your mind is in flames, bring it back to the present moment!

When you find yourself lying awake at night going over the things that have been done to you or entertaining fears of the future, just keep bringing your mind back to awareness of your breathing, perhaps of sounds outside the room, perhaps of the feel of the bedclothes. Don't worry about falling asleep or not, just keep coming back to the experience of the moment and you will be able to rest.

Guard your body

Eat and drink sensibly. Eat to maintain your health and strength even if you don't feel like eating. Watch out for overeating as a form of self-comforting. Also be aware of the dangers of drinking too much – among other things, alcohol gives people a false sense of control which can be very tempting if your power has been taken away by a bully. Drinking too much will simply reduce your ability to cope with the situation and will increase your feelings of depression the next day.

Take exercise. As well as being good for you physically, exercise has been proven to improve people's mood for some hours after they finish exercising. It also calms the mind. Exercise doesn't have to mean going to the gym – a brisk walk for twenty minutes to half an hour will leave you feeling better.

Play. Yes, play. Play is good for body and mind. If you have kids, play with them. If you like to play sports or going to movies, make sure you keep up these activities. Meet friends, have a laugh. These things 'take you out of yourself', as they say, and are hugely beneficial.

Remember: *there is more to you than what is going on in the job.*

TIP If you are being bullied at work, make safeguarding your own mental and physical health your top priority – and don't put it off until after you have dealt with the bullying.

The crusader trap

Chris was bullied by his immediate boss but the bullying has ceased following many complaints by Chris and his trade union. However, Chris wants the company to acknowledge that he was bullied and to punish his boss. The company has refused to do this. Chris has also been offered a very good severance package. He would like to take it but he feels that to do so would be to leave his work colleagues open to bullying. Meanwhile, Chris is on sick leave and veers between depression and anger every day.

Many people become locked in their bullying experience by falling into what I call the crusader trap. The crusader trap generally takes two forms:

1. Seeking revenge on the bullies and on the organisation that employs them
2. Refusing to leave the situation for the sake of your work colleagues.

Revenge

Revenge is not available. It is important to understand this. Hopefully, by making your case to the employer and the union you will be able to get the bullying stopped. That is about as much as you can hope for. Watch out for the desire for revenge: it will distort your judgement and your thinking and ruin your peace of mind. Actually, it will turn you into a would-be bully. Do you want that?

For the sake of the others

In the section on dealing with difficult people, above, I said that sometimes the only workable solution to a bad situation is to leave it. Some victims of bullying will not leave impossible situations, even when they have been made a good financial offer, because they feel they would be abandoning their work colleagues. In fact leaving, if that is what is needed for your own financial, mental and physical well-being, is the best possible example you could give your colleagues.

TIP Seeking revenge against your bully is almost certainly a waste of time. And staying in a bullying situation for the sake of your colleagues will do nothing for them and will damage you even further.

THIS CHAPTER'S TIPS

1. Never give responsibility for your physical and mental health to a bully.
2. If you are being bullied at work make safeguarding your own mental and physical health your top priority – and don't put it off until after you've dealt with the bullying.
3. Seeking revenge against your bully is almost certainly a waste of time. And staying in a bullying situation for the sake of your colleagues will do nothing for them but will damage you even further.

Note

1. Report of the Task Force on the Prevention of Workplace Bullying, Stationery Office, Dublin, 2001.

OUR PHYSICAL HEALTH

How we discount it and why

14

In this chapter
- Toughing it out
- Discounting the existence of the problem
- Discounting the importance of the problem
- Denying that anything can be done about the problem
- Denying that you personally can do anything about the problem

Toughing it out

Charlie was a good guy. His family loved him and he loved them. Couldn't do enough for them. But he wouldn't go to the doctor for a medical checkup unless his partner dragged him there – and getting him to agree to be dragged there was no easy thing. Even after he had a mild heart attack, Charlie missed appointments for checkups, worked long hours and generally disregarded what he saw as 'fussing'. Even when he got the chest pains that signalled the major heart attack that killed him, Charlie didn't do anything about them until the football match he was watching was over. Then he got into the car and drove himself to the hospital rather than bring a lot of 'fussing' down on his head by telling anybody about it. He died in the hospital car park.

Men get a bad press when it comes to health. While women's health has received enough attention for the past several decades to use up an entire rainforest of newsprint, there has been little enough in the media about men's health – apart, that is, from articles giving out to us for not taking good enough care of ourselves.

However, many of us, if not most of us, grew up in a culture in which we were expected to get on with things without making a fuss. The things we were expected to get on with included working exceptionally hard and, for some, going to war. In effect, men were expected to be tough guys and to get on with doing what needed doing regardless of its effect on health or well-being.

It is hardly surprising, then, that we bring these attitudes to our physical health. We have learned not to make a fuss – so we don't make a fuss about aches and pains, shortness of breath and other symptoms which perhaps we ought to be taking to the doctor. Even when the diagnosis of a condition has been made and even when that condition is serious we can, like Charlie above, still be tempted to tough it out. Again, all we are doing is engaging in a behaviour which is seen as a valuable male trait in other circumstances.

Unfortunately, the behaviour in question can have fatal consequences. Even when Charlie begins to have his final heart attack, he gets into his car, as do other men, and drives himself to the hospital. While he might be better advised to take an aspirin and wait for the ambulance, his default mode is to handle problems like this himself. The thing about a default mode is that, like a computer, we have a habit of going into it even when it is not the most helpful thing to do.

For as long as a society demands that men tough it out in other areas of their life, then the tendency will be to tough it out when it comes to health. When we do not take health issues seriously enough, we are discounting our health. This chapter, then, is about discounting. Let's make this clearer by looking at the four levels of discounting. Once we understand what's going on here, we have a better chance of spotting ourselves doing it and of stopping it.

The four levels are: discounting the existence of a problem; discounting the importance of the problem; discounting the possibility of anybody doing anything about the problem; and discounting our own personal ability to deal with the problem.

Discounting the existence of the problem

Frank is a farmer. This, naturally, involves him in a good deal of physical work. Lately, when Frank is working hard he experiences a heaviness in his chest. The heaviness goes away a short time after he stops working. This could be angina, which could be the first step towards a heart attack if not dealt with, but Frank takes the view that the heaviness is just tiredness, nothing more than that and nothing at all to be alarmed about.

The most basic level of discounting is to discount the existence of a problem. In other words, we simply refuse to accept that there is any problem at all. The smoker who declares that all this talk about smoking being bad for your health is nonsense is discounting the existence of a problem. Many an alcoholic has gone to his grave protesting that he does not have a drink problem of any kind whatsoever. Or consider the phenomenon of young men who race across the countryside at murderous speeds in souped-up cars and who will deny to anybody who asks that there is a problem with driving in this way. They drive well – people who crash do not – therefore they themselves do not have a problem.

Behind all this discounting, I suspect, is an attempt to defend a behaviour which might otherwise have to be given up. Denying that there is a problem at all enables the person to continue with the behaviour. So if the people closest to you are telling you that you have a problem and if you totally disagree with them, just allow yourself to consider for a moment whether they might be right.

TIP If other people are expressing concerns to you about the possible impact of a behaviour on your health, but you cannot see any validity whatsoever to these concerns, consider the possibility that you are discounting at the most basic level.

Discounting the importance of the problem

Terry knows he is 'a bit' overweight. He knows this because the doctor has told him so. Actually, the word used by his doctor was 'obese'. But Terry reckons his doctor only used this word in order to frighten him into going on a diet. 'That's doctors for you,' he laughs. 'They hate to see you enjoying yourself.'

Terry accepts that he has a weight problem but he denies that there is any importance to it. Other examples include the smoker who declares that he does not want to live to a ripe old age anyway, or the man who has a serious low back pain but who dismisses it as a twinge.

The person who discounts the importance of a problem is a step ahead of the person who discounts the existence of the problem in the first place. It is recognised in addiction treatment, for instance, that the person who discounts the importance of the problem is at least entering a potentially positive stage. This is the stage at which he might consider whether he needs to do something about it.

Discounting the importance of a health problem seems to be fairly common among men. If you look at women and men under fifty you will find that women are twice as likely as men to attend a doctor. But after fifty, men are twice as likely as women to be hospitalised. There is even some evidence that suggests that men who feel unwell will put off going to a hospital emergency department if they are watching an important football match.

Discounting the importance of a problem may also mask embarrassment. For instance, the man who finds it has become more difficult to pass urine may discount the importance of this symptom because he does not wish to undergo the embarrassment of the digital rectal examination for an enlarged prostate.[1]

TIP If you agree that you have a health issue but you deny that it is of importance, consider getting a professional opinion from the doctor who, after all, is paid to know more than you do about health problems.

Denying that anything can be done about the problem

Jack has pains in his arms and legs. He puts this down to age. What is the point in going to the doctor he asks? All the doctor can do is send him for tests which would only tell him what he knows already. He would have wasted time and money to no avail.

Most of us, once we accept that there is a problem, will do something about it. Let us be honest though: some of us will only do something about it after we have put off doing anything about it for quite a long time.

Putting off going to the doctor when we accept there is something wrong represents the third level of discounting and it is a pretty silly one. Sometimes it involves assuming that you know more than the doctors and all the specialists in the world. You know that all these people with their high-tech equipment and their training can do nothing. They may think they can do all sorts of things for you but it is they who are the fools and not you.

When you find yourself thinking this way, it is time to get yourself to the doctor. There is a good chance that what you have is different to what you think you have and that the doctors can do more for you than you think they can.

TIP If there is a problem, don't just sit there telling yourself there's nothing the doctor can do about it. You deserve better. Take the problem to the experts and give them a shot at it.

Denying that you personally can do anything about the problem
Michael's smoking has reached a point at which he is short of breath a good deal of the time. Friends have expressed fears that he might be at an early stage of emphysema. They want him to get into a smoking cessation programme, to try the various aids that exist and to have his health checked out by his doctor. But Michael argues that while these things may work for other people, they won't work for him. First, he is addicted to smoking and, second, he is more addicted than most people. He knows this because his father died from emphysema due to smoking. Smoking and emphysema 'run in the family'. There is nothing he can do about it.

This is the very last line of defence when it comes to discounting health problems. At this stage the person accepts that there is a problem, that it is an important problem and that, generally speaking, there is something that can be done about it. But he refuses to accept that anything can be done about it in his particular case.

This line of defence enables the person using it to continue his behaviour, in Michael's case smoking, even though he concedes that it is harming him. It is almost as though the pain of enduring the harm the behaviour will do to him is more acceptable than the pain of giving it up.

Most men, it should be said, have sought help before they reach that stage of denial, but it is a particularly sad stage of denial for those who go that far. It is as if the person is isolating himself from the help that could transform his life for the better.

Of course, it is not always a matter of going to doctors. It may be a matter of changing a behaviour yourself. Overeating is endemic in my family so there is no point in my going on a diet. Oh, yes? Prove it by going on a weight-loss programme – you might be pleasantly surprised.

TIP If you accept that there is a problem and that this problem is treatable for others, then assume it is treatable for you.

Men who discount their health problems not only die early but they live in more hardship than is necessary, enduring pain and discomfort that could be treated. They are not foolish men. Sometimes they are stubborn, sometimes afraid, sometimes just behaving the way society has told them to behave. But they are men who are loved and who will be missed when they are gone. They deserve to give themselves and their families another chance.

THIS CHAPTER'S TIPS

1. If other people are expressing concerns about the possible impact of a behaviour on your health, but you cannot see any validity whatsoever to these concerns, consider the possibility that you are discounting at the most basic level.
2. If you agree that you have a health issue but you deny that it is of importance, consider getting a professional opinion from the doctor who, after all, is paid to know more than you do about health problems.
3. If there is a problem, don't just sit there telling yourself there's nothing the doctor can do about it. You deserve better. Take the problem to the experts and give them a shot at it.
4. If you accept that there is a problem and that this problem is treatable for others, then assume it is treatable for you.

Note

1. Actually, you can ask your doctor to do a 'PSA test' which is non-invasive and simply involves taking a blood sample from your finger to check for possible prostate problems; testing for prostate trouble does not always have to be invasive unless the PSA test reveals the need for further investigation.

APPENDIX

The quick quick guide to key ideas in the book

Glance at this appendix now and then to refresh your memory on important concepts in this book. This quick 'refresher', which need take no more than a minute, will multiply the value you get from the book.

ACHE: In Choice Theory, the letters stand for four ways in which depression can 'hook' people: as a substitute for anger (A); as a way of gaining some control (C), however poor, over one's situation, usually in the form of avoidance; to get help (H) from others; and as an excuse (E) for not doing things we don't want to do, perhaps out of fear.

Acting out: Hitting, throwing and shouting when you feel bad. The antidote is to describe your feelings, i.e. explain why you feel bad, instead of expressing them in these ways.

All or nothing thinking: Assuming that because one thing is wrong everything is wrong, e.g. 'She lied to me once so I can never trust her again'. It is destructive of relationships and of peace of mind.

Anger management: A set of techniques which include noticing your physical feelings instead of getting caught up in angry thoughts; nipping your anger in the bud before it builds to a crescendo; and curbing the desire to control other people.

Awfulising: Telling yourself it will be 'awful' if such and such a thing happens or does not happen. Actually, most of our misfortunes are not awful at all: they are simply inconvenient.

Basic needs: The five needs common to all of us and that we always strive to meet, well or badly, according to Dr William Glasser's Choice Theory. They are Survival, Power, Belonging, Freedom and Fun.

Brooding: Thinking endlessly about things that have gone wrong. To be avoided, as it leads to depression.

Cart before the horse: We feel anxious or shy about many activities until after we have done them. To get things done, then, we need to put the cart (action) before the horse (feelings).

APPENDIX

Confusing meant and unmeant behaviour: Assuming that the things that annoy us are done deliberately for that purpose. The antidote is to practice the Recovery Inc slogan: people do things *that* annoy me not *to* annoy me.

Discounting: Refusing to acknowledge that a problem exists or that it matters or that anything can be done about it. Typically, men are seen as discounting physical health issues.

Disputing: A cognitive behavioural therapy technique in which you argue back when your mind tells you how terrible or upsetting various possibilities are or how bad you are. Very often, these thoughts are habits acquired as we grew up.

Exercise: Physical exercise is increasingly recognised as a mood-lifter which reduces depression. A brisk walk lifts the mood both during the walk and afterwards.

Extreme mental language: The habit of speaking to ourselves in extreme ways in our minds, e.g. 'You're a total disaster' or 'This is an absolute nightmare'. Such language is rarely justified and increases stress.

Fortune-telling: Wrongly assuming that you know what will happen in the future and that it will be bad is an important source of anxiety.

Gestures: A characteristic of healthy, long-term relationships is that couples get over arguments quickly. A gesture is a remark or act which signals that the argument is in the past. It could be as simple as asking your partner if they want something from the shop or giving them a kiss.

Gradual exposure: Very gradually exposing yourself to situations in which you feel afraid. Especially useful if you suffer from panic attacks or from the aftermath of a traumatic event.

Gratitude: Research shows that people who practice gratitude get on better in life and are happier than those who do not. Even a few minutes a day listing things big and small that you are grateful for can make a difference.

Hidden beliefs: Irrational beliefs which we are barely aware of but which strongly influence our lives. The top three, as identified by psychotherapist Dr Albert Ellis: I must do well and get the approval of everybody who matters to me or I will be a worthless person; people must treat me kindly and fairly – otherwise they are bad; I must have an easy, enjoyable life or I cannot enjoy living at all.

Insistence on being right: The insistence on being right at all times destroys relationships, as it leads to conflict over the smallest things.

Mediation: A service in which couples breaking up go to a mediator to agree issues concerning maintenance and custody. The aim is to avoid expensive and bitter legal battles and to reduce, as far as is practicable, the pain attached to the breakup.

Mind-reading: Assuming that you know what other people are thinking and that they are thinking negatively about you. Chances are, they are not thinking about you at all.

Mindfulness: An invaluable Buddhist technique in which you continually bring your attention back to what is going on at the present moment, instead of getting caught up in thoughts and memories. Mindfulness is helpful with anxiety, depression, panic attacks and many other issues.

Mirroring: When you see another person expressing a feeling such as anger or enjoyment, the brain cells linked to anger and enjoyment activate not only in their brains but in yours as well. You can use this phenomenon to improve relationships, for instance, by being positive around another person.

Morita Therapy: This Japanese approach advises three steps to dealing with anxiety: acknowledge that you are anxious, know what you need to do and do it anyway.

Naikan: A Japanese exercise in which we ask ourselves three questions to give us a more rounded view of another person. The three questions are: What have I received from this person? What has this person received from me? What troubles have I caused this person? There is no fourth question.

Optimism: According to Dr Martin Seligman's theory, optimism can be cultivated by giving yourself the credit for the things you do well, and by seeing your failures as due to specific, fixable behaviours (e.g. not studying for an exam) and not to flaws in your personality (e.g. stupidity).

Panic attacks: Feelings of fear, nausea, high heartbeat, breathlessness and other symptoms triggered by anxiety but often having no clear cause. In themselves, panic attacks are not physically harmful and normally peak after about ten minutes. But you should consult your GP to check that what you are having is a panic attack.

Paradoxical intention: An anxiety reduction technique in which you pretend you want something to happen that, in fact, you do not want to happen. For instance, a person who fears blushing in company might use this technique by telling himself that he intends to blush more brightly than anybody else in the room. The effect is to reduce anxiety.

Perfectionism: Based on the mistaken belief that getting something wrong would be catastrophic, perfectionism prevents us from taking action. In fact, most of the mistakes we make are far from catastrophic and are quickly forgotten.

Quality time: A brief period of time in which a couple engage in an activity which is positive for both of them. This could be as simple as a conversation or a walk during which they avoid discussing issues on which they are in conflict.

Quality World: In Choice Theory, your Quality World means all the things that matter to you, from trivial likes and dislikes to core values. Recognising that each person's Quality World is inevitably different is an important step in maintaining harmonious relationships.

Relationship stages: Almost all long-term relationships pass through three stages, namely infatuation, conflict and resolution. Resolutions can range from the breakup of the relationship to an acceptance by the couple of their mutual differences and a willingness to make the relationship better for both of them.

Secondary anxiety: Many situations, such as going for a job interview, create anxiety in themselves. This unavoidable level of anxiety is primary anxiety. Secondary anxiety is added unnecessarily by ourselves through telling ourselves how awful the experience is going to be.

Total Behaviour: In Choice Theory, this phrase refers to the four things that are going on for us at any one time. These are Doing, Thinking, Feeling and Physiological events. We have more control over what we *do* than over any of the other three.

RECOMMENDED READING

Choice Theory: A New Psychology of Personal Freedom, by Dr William Glasser, Harper Collins.

Don't Sweat the Small Stuff ... and it's all Small Stuff, by Richard Carlson, Hodder & Stoughton.

Feel the Fear and Do It Anyway, by Susan Jeffers, Random House.

Playing Ball on Running Water, by David K .Reynolds, Harper Collins.

The Couple's Journey, by Susan M. Campbell, PhD, Impact Publishers.

Wherever You Go, There You Are: Mindfulness Meditation in Everyday Life, by Jon Kabat-Zinn, Hyperion.